And Time Stood Still

The Conservative Congregant: Book Two

Paula D. Walker Baker

And Time Stood Still

First Paperback Edition, July 2016

ISBN-13: 978-0-6927422-0-4
ISBN-10: 0692742204

Library of Congress Cataloguing-in-Publication Data
Baker, Paula D. Walker
And Time Stood Still / Paula D. Walker Baker
Library of Congress Control Number: 2016948003

Cover Photo: Jacqueline E. Smith
Cover Design: Wind Trail Publishing

Printed in the United States of America.

For my church family, The Gathering, my husband, Stephen, my children, Amanda, David, and Micah, and their families with love.

"I am here. I am blessed. You are my brother."

Chapter 1

"How do you know you are my sister? You've never met me or at least you don't remember me," Gary questioned the lady sitting next to him.

"Because I have this," Eloise said, pulling the identical photo to his from her purse. "Mother gave this to me a few years before she died. She never told me who the guy was. I just assumed it was a cousin. I've never known I had a brother. Do you know why that might be? Where have you been? Where do you live? Are you on the streets?"

"Whoa!" Gary exclaimed, smiling. "One question at a time... I have lots of questions too. Like, why did Mother give you a photo of both of us and not tell you who I am? Did they ever talk about me? Where did you all move to? When did Mother die? Is Dad alive? Why are you here serving the food? This is all just so bizarre!"

"Well," Eloise said, "it's all kind of a long story about the meal and being down here at City of Hope Square. See, the priest who celebrates Mass here came to our church out in Poetry; I live in Poetry. Anyway, the priest told us about this congregation. Inadvertently, I volunteered to make the lunch for today. This was in February. I could have never known I'd meet you here this day, but I did hear from a good friend of mine that God blesses everyone mightily when they come down and worship here. I was a whole other person in February. You'd never believe it! Anyway, tell me some things about you. How old are you? I don't remember that photo being taken. Why was it taken? For what occasion?"

Gary took a bite of his meatloaf, savoring it as if he hadn't eaten in a while.

"This is how I remember Mom's meatloaf tasting. Is this her recipe?"

"Yes, I have all of Mom's recipes and this is one of my favorites."

"Mom was a great cook," they said simultaneously. Gary and Eloise looked at each other surprised and smiled.

"Wow, that was weird," Gary laughed

"Anyway, I guess I was about fifteen when I was sent away. I was a bit of a hooligan and they couldn't really handle me. I wanted them to just love me and I felt alone most of the time. I was a bad kid, but I never killed anyone, or anything like that. I just wanted them to pay attention to me. Instead, they sent me to Aunt Lulu's Did you know her?"

"No, I don't remember anyone named Lulu. I'm sure that would be a name I would remember. Lulu? Hmmm. Whose sister was she, Mom or Dad's?"

"Well, it turns out she wasn't a relative at all. Mom and Dad just used the word aunt because they were pretty close to her for some reason. I never got the full story of their relationship. Our family had so many secrets, it was hard to keep up with things that were true and the things that were made up."

Just at that moment, Edward walked up.

"Eloise, your meatloaf is superb, as usual, and you should hear the comments I'm hearing about the lunch. They love it! You have outdone yourself."

Eloise looked at Edward, her eyes intense.

"Oh, am I interrupting? I'm sorry."

"No, Edward. I don't know how to say this, but this is Gary. Turns out he's my brother," she said, almost flippantly, with a slight grin.

"Gary, this is Edward Dowager, my husband."

"Great to meet ya, man," Gary said, offering his hand to Edward.

"Oh, your brother! As in, 'we are all brothers and sisters in Christ.' Right?"

"Yes — no, that's not what I mean," she said, biting her lip and anticipating Edward's reaction. You remember that photo my mother gave me before she died, the one I carry around all the time with the unknown guy in it with me? Well, Gary is the guy in the photo!"

"How do you know?" Edward asked.

"Because he has the same photo! It dropped out of his pocket when he was in line for lunch. Can you believe it?"

"I didn't know you had a brother, Eloise," Edward stated suspiciously.

"Neither did I, but he showed me the photo and said the girl was his sister, and I'm that girl! I haven't found out what the story is yet. It seems he was sent away when he was about fifteen. That was about the time this photo was taken, but I don't remember him at all. He told me he was sent away to an Aunt Lulu's house somewhere. I haven't gotten the full details. We've only just started talking about it."

"Wow," he said. "Can you just come and check out the buffet for a minute, you know, to see how things are progressing?"

"Sure, no problem. Gary, I'll be right back. I am the person heading the lunch up, you know."

"Yes, go ahead. Take your time," Gary said, taking a bite of bread.

Her eyes flashed fire as Edward took her elbow and they walked away. She hated when he had done this a few times before when he was irritated. He was flustered and

3

surprised that Eloise would buy into this guy's story so readily.

"How do you know he is your brother? Is he a parishioner? I've never heard of Aunt Lulu and how do you know that he didn't just find that picture somewhere, anywhere? What do you know about him? This is weird and something just doesn't seem right, doesn't feel right."

"Well, I don't know anything yet except what he's told me. It's true... I don't remember any Aunt Lulu, who, by the way, wasn't a real aunt, just someone my family was close to. All I really know is that he and I have the same photo with the same people in it. How else would he know his sister's name was Eloise?"

"I don't know, honey, but he could have found that information anywhere. Does his picture have identification in the way of who it is in the picture?"

"Oh, I don't know. I didn't look or ask," she said.

While they were huddled together, Danielle came towards them and looking concerned, asked if Eloise was all right.

"Yes, I'm all right. Something really weird has happened and I'm not sure what to think about it."

"What do you mean?"

"Well, see that sandy-haired guy sitting by the alcove? He has a photo of me and him. It's the same photo that dropped out of my purse that day at The Well. Remember?"

"What? How can that be? How could he have one too?" Danielle asked.

"Well, I don't know. The thing is that his dropped out of his pocket and he said the little girl in the picture is his sister, Eloise!" I know that's me in the photo because of the copy I have, but how can I be sure that it's him in it with me? I mean, it's the very same photo. Edward thinks he could have found the photo anywhere, but if that were true, how would he know that the little girl's name was Eloise?"

Eloise panicked and her breathing became erratic. She grabbed her chest and then reached into her purse for her anxiety medication. This was not the time to have a panic attack. These panic attacks were becoming a bit of a nuisance, happening at the most inopportune times.

"The thing is, there is no way to check the facts. I mean, my parents are both gone now and there is no one to ask unless this "Aunt Lulu" is still alive. Also, I don't know if he is living on the streets or with a church or what. I don't know whether to leave him here and go home. I don't know what kind of person he is, so I don't want to invite a total stranger home with me. But, I don't want to lose him again in case he is my brother. What would you do?"

"Gosh," Danielle mused, "that's a tough one. I'm not sure what I'd do. I think I'd find out where he is staying and maybe make a coffee date or lunch date for you two to talk about things. What do you know about him?"

"Nothing much," Eloise said matter-of-factly, "not really. Just what he has told me about the Lulu woman and he was sent off to live with her because he was a hooligan no one could handle. Well, I've got to check on the buffet and then get back over to him. I don't want him to leave without me knowing where he is staying. Talk to you in a while."

Danielle ran her hand through her blond hair and exhaled forcefully.

"Oh boy," she muttered under her breath.

Eloise went to check on the buffet and announced there was enough for seconds. People flocked to the table to be first to get the second helping. It was a great lunch on a beautiful day. It was not too hot, just a perfect day for a supernatural blessing from God. She wondered if Gary were her blessing, her miracle. She drew in a deep breath and blew it out slowly, with purpose.

With her head reeling from the news of a brother, she went back to the alcove and sat with Gary.

"Gary, are you on the streets?"

"I have been before, but now I'm staying with some friends for a while. I've been trying to turn my life around. I am going to Alcoholics Anonymous and I'm looking for a job. It's not been an easy life and it's been my fault. I have been mixed up in drugs and drinking but have finally quit doing drugs altogether. I do still have a problem with drinking. You know that runs in the family, right?"

"If I didn't before, I do now," Eloise acknowledged. "I know Dad drank a good deal, but he never really seemed drunk. At least, I don't think so."

"He was always drunk. That was how he lived; he was a functional alcoholic. That's why I was such a handful. He was mean to me and always yelled at me. I felt unwanted most of the time. Mom tried to make up for it, but she was no match for him."

Eloise's mouth dropped at his description of their dad. The man he described was not the man Eloise remembered. She remembered a man who let her sit on his lap, laughed with her, played with her, let her help him work on the old '48 Ford. He was everything to her and Gary was describing a stranger. She told him as much.

"Well, then you were lucky," he said. "That was all I ever wanted in a dad; someone who would play ball with me, help me with my school projects, just love me because I was his, you know? But, that never happened for me and I guess it was my fault. At least that was how it felt. I am glad, though, you had a different experience than I did; it really did a number on me. I would never want that for you."

Eloise wondered how it could be that Dad was so different for her than for Gary. What was the reason? How could she have missed so many things Gary picked up on? How could her dad have fooled her so completely and why didn't her mom fill her in on things? She began to think her whole life was a lie. At least that's what it felt like at this exact moment. Eloise took a breath and decided to reserve her judgments until she found the truth.

Chapter 2

As the afternoon wound down and the parishioners finished their lunches, Eloise, Gary, and Edward sat huddled together, talking and laughing as if old friends. Even so, Edward still had his reservations. But, he hoped to catch something in Gary's stories to negate the familial connection. He just couldn't believe they came to serve lunch and found her "brother."

I believe in miracles, I guess, Edward thought, *but really?*

Eloise's voice brought him back to the here and now.

"Gary, I have to help clean up the lunch buffet and table before we go home. Do you think there is a time this week when we might be able to meet up and talk some more? Do you have a cell phone? I'd like to have a way to get in touch with you before we part."

He looked at her, smiled and said, "I don't have a cell phone, but my friend does. I don't think he'll mind if I give you the number and you give me yours, too, okay?"

Gary had such a warm smile. It reminded Eloise of her dad's smile. Her dad, Matthew J. Remick, was a man who could charm his way around anything and Gary reminded her of that fact. It was quite odd that this man, who may or may not be her brother could remind her so much of her dad. But, he did. She was secretly happy about it and felt a certain comfort from it as well. She and her dad had been very close.

They exchanged phone numbers and promised each other to call by Tuesday to set up a time and place to get together. She hugged him and went back to the buffet table to begin cleaning up with Danielle and Kathy.

Andrew, one of the parishioners, brought the huge trash bin to the buffet area and the girls began to throw things away. They blew out the Sterno that kept the food warm and packed up unused items. There were some hygiene packs left over and those were given to The City of Hope leaders to pass out as needed. Waiting for the buffet warmer to cool down a bit, Eloise, Kathy, and Danielle began to talk while they worked.

"Who is that guy I saw you talking with, Eloise?" Kathy inquired.

It would be something she would learn to explain to others about, so she drew a deep breath and told Kathy about Gary. Kathy's eyes widened as Eloise told the story about how the two had met. It was, after all, hard to believe Eloise didn't remember her brother and they held onto the same photo their mother had given them. What are the chances of that ever happening to anyone? This must be her blessing!

"Oh my gosh, Eloise!" Kathy exclaimed, a huge smile on her face. "How do you feel about all this?"

"I am not sure I know how to feel about it," Eloise answered. "I mean, I kind of feel like my parents betrayed me, I guess. I'm not sure that's the word I mean, but it's the closest one I can think of. I can't wait to find out more details and try to find this Lulu woman. I wonder if Gary is still in contact with her or if she is still alive?"

"I don't know," Danielle interjected, "but it is going to be awesome to see how this is all going to pan out."

As soon as the buffet warmer cooled down, they packed it up and were then on their way back to Eloise's house in Poetry.

Once there, Eloise offered the girls tea and pulled out thank you gifts for both of them.

"I couldn't have pulled this off without you guys. Thank you so much for all your help and hard work. I really don't think it could have gone any better or been more fun and it's thanks to you two."

"Awww," Kathy and Danielle said at the same time, "You didn't have to do this; it was our pleasure," they agreed.

They sat around the table sipping their tea and the conversation turned toward Gary.

"What are you going to do about Gary?" Danielle asked.

"Do? What do you mean, do? What can I do? I'll have to sort out if he really is my brother and I think I know just the way to do it."

"How? Kathy wondered.

"Well, you know, DNA tests are quite popular and I would imagine if they can tell about other relatives, they could tell about siblings. Whether Gary will consent to it or not, I don't know. But, I think I'll call the doctor or whoever I need to call and find out about the tests tomorrow. What do you all think? Think that would be offensive to Gary?"

"Well, I think if it turns out to offend him, then something may not be right," Danielle stated matter-of-factly. "I mean, if he's the real deal, why would he mind?"

Eloise, scratching her chin, agreed. "I just want to know for sure. I mean, it's kinda weird to find a relative in a place like The City of Hope and not run a test to find out if it's true. I don't mean that like it must sound, but it is, at the very least, different."

"I told you when you leave your own comfort zone for God's purpose, things happen! It's amazing that it happens every time!" Danielle gushed. She was so happy about this surprise reunion she could just burst. She thought the reunion to be one of God's greatest ideas yet.

The two women finished their tea and headed toward the door, each off to their own houses for an afternoon nap. Eloise thought she might take a nap too. It had been a long day, one she had anticipated for a long time now and with Gary showing up, well, it was all just a bit overwhelming.

She drifted off to a fitful sleep quickly. All the information Gary had given her about the father he'd known swirled in her head even as she slept. After forty-five minutes, she opened her eyes, took a deep breath, and exhaled forcefully. She lay on her bed for just a few minutes, trying to sort things out. She then wondered where Edward was and what he was doing. She needed to be with him just now. He was always so comforting for her. Yes, that's just what she needed.

Eloise found Edward on his red riding mower in the front yard. He loved to work outside and she could always find him in his yard, mowing or pulling weeds or planting. Most of the gardeners in her neighborhood were women. Eloise smiled to herself when she thought of all the plants she had killed trying to make them grow. But, Edward? He was a natural. Everything he touched grew beautifully. It was hot outside, so she decided to take him a lemonade. She even put a little umbrella in the glass to make it special for him. She thought he would think it silly and she liked doing things that were a little out of character for her. Since she'd been going to The City of Hope, it'd been like that for her.

Edward saw Eloise and the umbrella-laden lemonade and stopped the mower.

"Well, what's the occasion, my dear? he asked, with a broad smile across his face.

"Heat. That's the occasion! It's hot out here; you're mowing and you have no drink in sight," she giggled. "Here, I've made a little lemonade for you. Want to come sit and drink it?"

"Sure, I could take a little break, but don't tell my wife. She works me to death, you know." He flashed a sarcastic, sideways smile.

"Seriously? And she doesn't help you? Wow, she sure is mean!" she joked back.

All kidding aside, Edward saw the look in Eloise's eyes.

"Are you okay, honey? I know this has been a stressful, overwhelming day for you. How are you doing?"

"You're right, Eddie, it really has been quite the day. I really needed to just be out here with you to calm down a bit and get your take on things."

She hadn't called him "Eddie" in years. It used to be a pet name, but since she had become so conservative and staid, she hadn't used it. But, she had changed lately and while it was for the good, it was almost unsettling to him.

The City of Hope and its people sure have been good for her, he thought.

She had loosened up a great deal and seem more relaxed, without the aid of more anti-anxiety meds. But, she seemed particularly vulnerable now. He knew she hated feeling vulnerable and it usually put her on edge. She seemed to embrace that vulnerability this time, though.

It was his job to protect her and this time, he was sure she needed that protection even more now. The whole thing was amazing.

The redwood patio furniture was comfortable and it was nice to look out over the yard and smell the newly mown grass. The fragrance was heady and made Eloise feel like a kid on summer vacation. She loved the smells of summer and it always took her back to her own backyard at her parents' house. Yet, here she was in her own yard experiencing those same feelings.

Edward sat close enough to her to hold her hand while he sipped his lemonade.

"Didn't you get any lemonade for yourself?"

11

"No, but I should," Eloise said as she got up to get a glass.

She returned shortly, lemonade in hand and sat next to her husband.

"Eddie, I'm just not sure what to think about Gary. I'm fairly certain he's my brother. But, the only way I can be sure is to have a DNA test performed on each of us. What do you think about that?"

"I think that's a good idea. It will definitely answer your questions one way or the other. Do you think it's something Gary is willing to do?"

"I don't know why he wouldn't," Eloise worried aloud. "I mean, it will give a definitive answer as you said, but do you think it would offend him? I don't want him to think I think he's lying to me, yet I don't know why I'm so worried about offending him."

"Well, if he does, that's kind of his problem, isn't it?" Edward surmised.

"I just don't want to start out on the wrong foot with someone who may be my brother," she replied.

"I know you don't want to hear this, Eloise, but I think the whole thing is kind of weird. I mean, you don't remember a brother and your mother never told you about one. Now this guy drops a photo of you and someone and he wants you to think he's your brother? Who is he trying to kid?"

"But, Edward, we don't know it's a scam and I think if we have the DNA tests performed, the answer will be clear. I'm going to call the doctor or lab or whoever does these things tomorrow and find out how to get one done."

"Okay, I'm just trying to watch out for you. I don't want you to get hurt in this process. If he is your brother, he might have had a whole different life than you did. So, I'm just asking you to be careful and guard yourself," he said.

"I know it's a strange thing, but I feel some kind of connection to Gary and it's something I just can't explain. I can't imagine God would bring this man to The City of Hope to pull a scam on me. He just wouldn't do that," she said matter-of-factly.

Chapter 3

In the morning, Eloise made a list of things she wanted to accomplish. She thought lists were great and she felt a strong satisfaction in crossing items off one by one. She wanted to tidy the house up and make her phone calls most of all. She had some piddly little things she wouldn't mind getting done if she had the time and patience for it, but it wasn't necessary to finish them today.

Her first call was to Gary. She knew it was still early, but she wanted to make sure she caught him at home. She pulled his number out of her purse and dialed. She was startled when a female answered the phone with a sleepy "Hello?"

"Hi, my name is Eloise Dowager and I'm looking for Gary Remick. Is he there by any chance?"

"Gary? Oh! Gary. Hold on, I'll see if he is awake," the voice said.

"Hello?"

"Gary? Hi, this is Eloise. Did I wake you?"

"Uh, a little bit, but it's okay. What's up?"

"Well," Eloise began, "I wanted to see if you were up to getting together sometime this week. There is a lot I want to talk to you about and I'm sure you have some questions for me, too."

"Yeah, I'd like that," his voice strong now. "Just tell me when and where and I'll be there."

"It depends on what you want to do. What is your pleasure? Coffee or lunch?" she inquired.

"Lunch sounds good. Are you talking about today or when?"

"Do you want to meet today? I have the afternoon open, so, it's a possibility," she said softly.

"I was going to look for a job, but I can put it off until tomorrow," Gary stated.

"Gary, do you have an appointment with someone or anything like that?"

"No, nothing like that; I was just going to look in the paper and go to the unemployment office, so it's cool."

"Where do you live," Eloise asked, realizing she had forgotten that he was in Dallas.

"I'm at the Kookaburra Apartments on Empire Central," he answered.

Eloise heard herself gasp. She knew that area and it wasn't a good one. One of her friend's daughters had lived around there. The daughter finally saved enough money to get out. She knew liquor and drugs were easy to get there. With him being an alcoholic, it couldn't be easy for him to live there with temptation all around him.

"Eloise, are you still there?" Gary prodded.

"Oh, sorry. I know right where you are. Shall I come pick you up around noon?"

"Sure, I'll be ready. I can't wait to see you again," he said excitedly.

"Hey Gary, can I ask you to be waiting outside for me? I really don't like that area. It scares me."

"Oh yea, of course," Gary replied. "You're right, it's not a great area to live."

"Okay, see you then. Bye."

"Okay, bye."

Chapter 4

I really dread going into that part of town. I wish he lived anywhere but over on Empire Central.

Eloise tried not to think about it and just got in her car at eleven-fifteen for the forty-five-minute drive into Dallas. She turned on the Christian radio station and began drumming on the steering wheel to the beat of the music. Pretty soon, she exited Empire Central and drove through the seedy neighborhood to the Kookaburra Apartments. As promised, Gary stood by the entrance waiting for her. He jumped in the car and they drove off.

"I want to take you to The Mecca. It's a diner over on Harry Hines that makes home-cooked food. Oh man! They make the best bread pudding too. Does that sound okay to you?"

"Sure, anywhere you want to go is fine with me," he remarked.

The car was filled with a deafening silence. Neither one knew what to say to the other. Eloise hoped when they got to the diner, they would both loosen up. The veil of quiet hanging in the atmosphere was awkward and Eloise didn't know how to break it. She didn't do well with awkwardness. She just hoped she wouldn't have a panic attack.

The small parking lot at the Mecca was full, as usual. This place was one of the best places to eat and everyone in

Dallas knew it. Finally, Eloise was able to squeeze into a parking space.

"This is one of the best places to eat in Dallas," Eloise informed Gary. "You're going to love it!"

"I'm pretty hungry," Gary offered, "so I probably will."

The diner was full and they had to wait about five minutes for a table, but Eloise knew it would be worth the wait. Besides, it was just past noon and loads of people who worked in the area ate here. The wait was never very long. They were taken to a table where Eloise and Gary both ordered Dr. Peppers. They laughed about their tastes being the same.

They sat looking at each other as if to find some clue as to why they were separated all those years ago. But, the only story in Gary's dark eyes seemed to be sadness. Finally, Eloise spoke up. "How old are you? I'm fifty."

"I'm sixty-three, thirteen years older than you. Remember, I was fifteen in that photo and you were two."

"I remembered, but I really didn't know how old I was in the picture. Mom just gave me the photograph with no explanation. It was really weird because she wouldn't say who you were other than 'a friend.' Where did you get the photo from and when?"

Gary began, "Well, one day, Aunt Lulu got a package in the mail and the picture was in the package. I know there was a family Bible, but I didn't know who it was from or anything. After she opened it and read the letter, she gave me the picture and told me the little girl was my sister. I'd remembered I had a sister, but I didn't know much about her. I remember it made me feel kind of alone and sad that I didn't know you. It was just me and Lulu, you know, and it was kind of lonely not having any brothers or sisters around. Of course, I never had any brothers, but you know what I mean."

"Yep, I sure do," her voice trailing off as her thoughts took over. Snapping herself out of it, she carried on with her questions.

"Is Aunt Lulu still alive and if she is, how old is she?"

"Yeah, she is, actually," he started, "but she's in a nursing home. She has some dementia. It's odd because sometimes, she doesn't remember much, but other times, she's clear as a bell. I guess she is in her mid-eighties by now."

"Do you think she might remember why you were sent to her, what had transpired? And did you ever look in that family Bible for any clues?" If the photo came with that package, then it must have been from Mom."

"Oh, you know, I never even thought of that. I wasn't very much older than the photo when the package came and so I didn't think much of it. But, you're right, there might be a clue in the Bible. The thing is, I'm not sure where it is now. Aunt Lulu, though, is at The Village Nursing Center in Richardson and we could go for a visit if you wanted."

"Oh, that sounds intriguing," Eloise gushed. "I feel like Nancy Drew," she giggled.

He rolled his eyes at his little sister and laughed.

"Gary, I have to ask you, and I don't want you to be offended, but what would you think about getting a DNA test done? That would tell us definitively whether we were brother and sister." Eloise bit her lip waiting for his response.

There was a pregnant pause, while he exhaled and pushed his hair out of his eyes. "Sure, I don't see why not. I mean, I can understand you wanting to have the test done. A perfect stranger has a photo of you and it does seem kind of weird, after all," he rambled.

"No, well, nothing against you or anything," Eloise suggested. "I'm just saying since we don't know the story, a DNA test might give us the base we need to sort the details out. Because there is a story here. So, it's nothing other than to tell us if we are truly the people in this photo. That's all."

"Look, Eloise, it's fine with me. I can understand and I'd like to find out what the tale behind all this is too. Yes, I'd like to have the test done. I just don't want you to think I pick people at random and claim to be their brother." And with that he laughed.

Eloise was glad that he could be somewhat lighthearted about it all. She hadn't wanted to offend him in any way and by suggesting the test, well, that left it open for interpretation.

The waitress brought their food. Gary ordered the chicken fried steak, with mashed potatoes and green beans while Eloise ordered the pot roast with mashed potatoes and carrots. It was her favorite dish there.

"Can I get you anything else?" the waitress asked.

At the same time, both Eloise and Gary asked for iced water. They laughed about the coincidence. Those were becoming more and more frequent.

"What was it like growing up with Aunt Lulu, Gary?"

"I don't know, probably no different than growing up anywhere else. Dad and I didn't get along, so I didn't have to contend with his badmouthing me or yelling at me. Aunt Lulu actually was a good surrogate mother. She didn't work outside the house so I had her all to myself whenever I needed her. I had already begun drinking before I left home and I supposed that was one of the reasons they sent me away. I don't know. There was never really any discussion as to why I was being sent away, so I always just figured it was because I was always drinking and not a good influence on you or anyone else."

"That's just so sad they didn't even talk to you about it. They didn't talk about you to me at all. I just was talking to Mom one day and she gave me the photo and said it was me when I was a little girl. It was all really weird. I know you said you and Dad didn't get along, but it wasn't that way for me. I don't even know if I was aware he drank."

"How could you not know he was a drunk?"

"He never acted drunk to me," Eloise explained. "He was always just, well, Daddy.

"Hmm, weird," Gary mused.

"Not changing the subject or anything, but when would you be able to do the DNA test? Do you have a specific time that, you know, one time that's better than the other?" Eloise wondered.

"No, not really. Since I'm not working or anything just now, I'm pretty much open most of the time. I do have AA meetings at noon most days. I try to go to as many meetings as I can, especially considering where I live. So, just set it up for a time that is convenient for you. No worries."

"Okay," Eloise answered, "After I drop you off at home and I get home, I'll call whoever I need to call and set up an appointment. I think it's just a cheek swab, so no needles or anything, which is good for me since I'm afraid of needles," she laughed.

"Me too!" Gary laughed. "Hate the things!"

They finished eating, paid the tab, leaving a generous tip and headed towards Gary's apartment. Once again, Eloise was nervous about being back in this neighborhood, but since Gary was with her, it was okay for the time being. But, the minute he got out of the car, she sped off toward the highway.

Chapter 5

The first thing Eloise did when she got home was kick off her shoes. She hated shoes and would much rather be barefoot. It sure did feel good to get rid of them. She threw her purse on the counter and went directly to the coffee pot, made a cup, and called her doctor's office.

"Hi, this is Eloise Dowager and I'm trying to find out how to go about getting a DNA sibling test. Do I have to get a prescription from Dr. Drew to have the test done?"

"No, ma'am. Since we live in Texas, you would just go to a lab to have the test performed; no prescription is needed. You can find a lab or you can use the lab we recommend. Which do you prefer?"

"I'm not familiar with this kind of thing, so if you know of one, I'd appreciate if you could just send me to the one you all use," Eloise said thoughtfully.

"Okay, it would be Dallas Genetic Lab over on Inwood Road."

The receptionist gave her the phone number and Eloise thanked her and hung up. Eloise took a sip of her coffee and a deep breath before she picked her phone up and dialed once again. This time, she called Dallas Genetic Lab to set up the appointment. Her hand trembled a little while she dialed. She didn't know why she was so nervous. She was slightly afraid of what she may find out with this test. Trying to calm herself, she thought, *Well, he's either my brother or he's not and this will be the deciding factor.* But, she had already connected with him on some level, so what would happen, she wondered, if he wasn't any relation at all?

"Dallas Genetic Lab, this is Teresa, may I help you?"

"Hi, I was wondering how to go about getting an appointment for a DNA sibling test for my brother and I?"

"Well, you would just make an appointment for a cheek swab and if there were no complications with the test, your result will be ready as soon as four to five days. Are you interested in making an appointment now?"

"Yes, I think so. What is the earliest appointment you have for tomorrow?" Eloise asked.

"I have a ten o'clock open for tomorrow."

"That would be perfect, I think. I'll take that, thanks."

"And your name, ma'am?"

"Oh, sorry. Dowager, Eloise Dowager. Do you need my brother's name?"

"Sure, what is his name?"

"Gary Remick," she answered.

"Okay, Mrs. Dowager, I have you down for ten o'clock tomorrow morning."

"All right," she said pleasantly. "See you then."

Eloise hung up the phone and called Gary's number.

Gary answered the phone, "Hey, Eloise."

"Hey. I've made an appointment at Dallas Genetic Lab for tomorrow at ten o'clock. Are you game?"

"Sure," he replied, "The sooner, the better!"

"Okay, then!" she exclaimed. "It's over there on Inwood Road, not too far from you, so I'll be there at nine fifteen. Okay?"

"Okay, see you then!" Gary hung up and Eloise took a deep breath, exhaled, and whispered, "Okay."

Later on that evening, Edward came home and Eloise told him all about the lunch and the appointment for the DNA testing.

"Sounds like you had a full day, a rather emotional one at that. How are you doing, hon?" he asked tenderly.

"Well, I think I'm okay, I'm pretty wiped out, though. You're right, it has been an emotional day. I don't know why, but when I was dialing the number to the genetics lab, my hands trembled so much. I was just so nervous. Maybe I have connected so closely to Gary that I am worried he's not my brother. I've never had a brother and now that he's here, I quite like it. Does that make sense?" she asked.

Edward knew what she meant because of his own brother. It was nice to have a brother, a co-conspirator, a partner in crime, someone to turn to when you need somebody to understand as only a brother can. He nodded his head, "Yes, Eloise, it makes perfect sense. It must feel a bit odd, though, for you to have a brother after all these years of being the only child."

"It has been really weird, but it has also felt so natural. Like I've always known him. Why do you think that is?" she wondered.

"It could be that somewhere deep down, you remember him being with you and your family. It may not be a conscious thing. It may be buried way down, but it is there. It must be," he replied.

"Maybe so," Eloise's voice trailed off as she looked at nothing in particular. "Hmm," she said quietly.

Chapter 6

The next morning, Eloise was up bright and early as if it was Christmas morning. Her eyes flung open at five a.m. and she couldn't go back to sleep. She got up, made coffee, and prepared breakfast for Edward and herself. That was an unusual undertaking. Most days, Edward microwaved a sausage and biscuit and called it breakfast. He was happy to make it since he didn't want to inconvenience his wife. She did a lot for him and he liked to let her sleep late, if she didn't have to be anyplace special. But, this morning, he was elated to have breakfast waiting for him when he got out of the shower.

"Thank you, darlin', for fixing my breakfast. It's a rare treat, indeed."

"I know," she said, remorsefully. "I should make it every day. That's what wives are supposed to do," she added.

"Naw, I'd rather let you have your beauty sleep. There are other things you do for me that are more important," he smiled.

Eloise smiled back and then looked out the window at the lawn. She caught herself daydreaming and then went to sit with Edward at the table. She had to admit waking up early was kind of nice, but then reasoned it wasn't really for her.

It was still a few hours until she would have to leave to pick Gary up for the test. She decided she would work the crossword puzzle. She could check her email, but no one really ever emailed her, so she felt it was a waste of her time.

"So, Edward, what if this DNA test comes up positive that he's my brother? Do I then, oh, I don't know, invite him out to the house for dinner? I don't know what it would mean."

"Eloise, why don't we wait for the results before we start inviting him over and such as that. I mean, these are all things we'll have to consider and talk about. We just need to pray about all of it. That is the only way we are going to know what exactly we need to do. God will lead the way; we just have to remember to let Him."

"All right, then. Thank you for reminding me to pray about it. I forget that I am unable to control everything, no matter how much I'd like to," Eloise laughed. "And I would like to!"

Finally, it was time for Eloise to head toward Gary's apartment to pick him up. She turned on the Christian radio station, like always, and began singing the song currently playing. The music always made her feel hopeful and cheerful. She felt it started her day off on the right foot. It was difficult to have a bad day when it starred with God; that was her motto. She thought back to the time she and Danielle had lunch at The Well and she had had a panic attack because she felt she could never be close to God.

My, how things have changed. And all because of The City of Hope and coming out of my comfort zone.

She pulled into the driveway of Gary's apartments and he, waiting on her, jumped in the car, raring to go.

"Hey, sis," he said sprightly.

Eloise was taken aback at the greeting. She smiled at him and said, "Hey you." Secretly, it made her nervous. What if they weren't siblings? She was trying to stay at arm's length even though she was just thinking about the blessings from coming out of her comfort zone.

"Everything okay?" Gary asked.

"I think so. I'm just a little nervous about the test, I guess. I mean, aren't you, just a little?"

"Not really. It's just a swab and then it will be over," he said, cheerfully. "Why are you nervous?"

"I guess it's just all the implications of being or not being brother and sister. I feel like I've bonded with you in some way and I don't know, I think it would be almost devastating to find out we aren't related. On the other hand, if we are related, what does that mean for us? We've been apart most of our lives."

"I don't know. I mean, I know what you are saying, but I really feel like we'll know what to do when we find out the results. It could be a great adventure," he quipped.

It didn't take them long to get over to Inwood Road. Eloise spotted the lab, so they parked and went in.

After filling out the necessary paperwork, it wasn't a very long wait. Their cheeks were swabbed and the appointment was over.

"The results should be ready in four to five days barring no complications. They will be mailed to you directly and you can look it up online," the nurse informed them.

Gary and Eloise looked at each other and nodded their heads. "Oh, you mean we don't come back here for the results?" asked Eloise.

"No, we never give the results in person," she said.

"Good," they said at the same time. Eloise looked at Gary and said, "That's good to know." They smiled at each other and Eloise playfully said, "Let's get lunch!"

"Okay," Gary agreed. With that, they hustled out of the building and to the car.

Gary and Eloise talked about possible places to eat and Gary offered, "I know a place over on Harry Hines; The

Blue Plate Diner. It's kind of an old place, but the food is really good and of course, they have the Blue Plate Specials. It's an amazing place."

"All right," Eloise instructed, "You'll have to tell me how to get there. Let me know well in advance so that I don't miss a turn or anything." Eloise was always so particular about some things

They arrived at The Blue Plate Diner, ate lunch, and lingered a bit, drinking coffee and talking. It was as if they wanted to stay together as long as they could because they'd been apart for so long. They had so much to talk about. Gary talked about his life with Aunt Lulu and Eloise talked about her life with her parents. She didn't talk about them to make Gary feel jealous or to make him feel bad. Rather, she talked about her life in comparison to what he experienced with her parents. She talked about her dancing lessons, archery lessons, and other privileges she'd had and he told her that Aunt Lulu put him in karate classes to channel his pent up energy somewhere. He liked the classes and took them until he was a black belt.

"What was Aunt Lulu like?" Eloise asked.

Gary began slowly, "She was always very kind to me; sadly, I can't say I was always kind back. She was a heavy-set woman with black hair that had streaks of silver right up at the top, where I guess her bangs or whatever were. Anyway, she was a bit squatty; to me, she looked just like a Lulu would look. She had a good sense of humor and she laughed a lot. In fact, that was her answer to everything; she would just laugh. I think it was a kind of nervous response to things. But, she was fiercely protective of me. She didn't let people mess with me, that's for sure. She did the best she could by and for me, but I was not always what I should have been. As I grew up, I had more respect for her and we talked about Mom and Dad sometimes, but, I think she thought talking about them hurt me more than it helped.

27

Sometimes it did hurt. I could not understand why I had to come live with Lulu, but it wasn't a bad life."

"I'm so glad to hear that, Gary. I'm happy to hear you were with Lulu, who gave you some good opportunities and even though the laughing was probably a nervous tic-like thing, she taught you to laugh and that is so good. That's not a trait everyone has. Since going to the City of Hope Square, I've laughed more than I ever had. Before going to that church, I was just a stuffy middle-aged woman who had to have everything just so. That's not me anymore. I've had friends pray for me. I've prayed for me and God knows Edward has probably prayed I'd get sorted out and it's happened. I've lightened up in so many ways." With that, she flashed a beautiful smile. The smile slowly faded away and Eloise said seriously, "Still, I wonder what life might have been like if we had grown up together."

"I don't know," Gary said.

And they collected their bill, paid, and left for home in silence.

The ride to Gary's apartment was uneventful and after dropping him off, Eloise went to the grocery store and then back home. She was glad to be home. She loved hanging out with Gary, but it sure did drain her emotionally. It wasn't any one thing in particular that seemed to zap her energy. Rather it was really just the whole situation. She hoped after the results of the DNA test came back, she would settle into a more stable place within herself. Then, she thought, she might calm down. She sure did hope so. All of this uncertainty was definitely taking its toll on her. She went to her room and laid down on the bed only to fall asleep in a few minutes. She must have been more exhausted than she thought; it was two hours later when she woke up.

She thought about Danielle and decided to call her. She hadn't really had much of a chance to talk to her about Gary and the DNA testing and everything since it all started.

She dialed the number and waited for an answer. Instead, she got Danielle's voice mail and began leaving a message.

"Hi, Danielle. It's Eloise. I'm sorry I've seemed so distant lately, just been so busy. Call me when you get home and let's catch up. Ta-ta dahlink."

The message made Eloise smile. She loved to call people "Dahlink." Sometimes, she just felt like being silly and she felt like that was something badly needed just now.

Chapter 7

It was early evening when the phone rang. Because Eloise and Edward were in the middle of dinner, they let voicemail pick it up. Eloise couldn't help but giggle when she heard the cheerful voice of her friend, Danielle say, "Tag! You're it! Call me back." She couldn't wait to talk to her friend and tell her about Gary and the cheek swab and the drives to Empire Central, Lulu and all the other stuff that was going on in her life now. There were times she felt overwhelmed, but for the most part, those times were few and far between. It seemed as though her panic attacks had even been less frequent. She felt a different kind of life breathing within herself now and she wondered if it was Gary, the church, the meal, or what? It was like the excitement of going to a carnival at night with all the lights shining brightly. Only the light was inside her. It felt as if it had taken over her body and her mind. It was exciting and daunting all at the same time.

It was eight o'clock that evening before Eloise had a chance to call Danielle back. They were so excited to talk to each other, they sounded like little birds chirping. Edward looked toward Eloise and offered the smile of all husbands loving the sound of their wives having fun.

Eloise told Danielle about the lunches she and Gary had had, how she had made the appointment at the DNA laboratory and how she was excited and yet, scared. Danielle could feel the tension in her voice and reassured her friend.

"It will all be over in just a couple of days and you will know what the relation is between the two of you. I know it has to be nerve wracking just now, but just think. You may have the brother you've wanted all this time!"

"I know," Eloise concurred, "but even that is just beyond my wildest imagination. Maybe I should go to a shrink to adjust to all of this," she said jokingly.

Danielle's voice was serious, "You know, Eloise, that wouldn't be a bad idea. You may be able to sort out why you don't remember anything about him. Two years old is very young, but, well, maybe I'm just grasping at straws here. I don't know. All I'm saying is maybe there is a reason you don't remember."

"Well, could be, but I choose to think it's just because I was so young. I mean, I don't know many people who remember when they were two. Three, maybe, but two? Nah." And the subject was changed. Danielle knew the tone in Eloise's voice and it meant she no longer wanted to discuss the possibilities of her memory or the lack thereof.

The two talked a bit longer about this and that, and then agreed to talk when Eloise got the results back from the DNA lab.

Edward sat in his favorite chair, a rust-colored, leather recliner he had received for his birthday last year. If he wasn't outside, one could always find him in his chair. Eloise sat on the tan leather chaise lounge. She did most of her thinking on that lounge. This time, she chewed her cuticles as she sat there.

Edward watched her for a minute or two and then said, "You know, you are going to make your fingers sore if you chew your cuticles. You always do. What's up?"

"I don't know, Eddie. There are just so many questions I have for Gary. Regardless of the test results, I just have lots of questions and I want to find some answers. I

31

want to find this Lulu lady and I want to find the family Bible that Mother sent to her. I want to know why I was never told about my brother — if he is my brother. If he's not, I want to know why he has the photo like the one Mother gave me. Where did he get it?"

"Well, now, Eloise, you know those answers will come. Maybe not when you want them to, but you'll have the answers when it is time and when you can handle it. God's timing is always perfect and you can want answers until the cows come home, but it's gotta be in God's timing. Now, I know that's not what you want to hear exactly, but for now, you're just gonna have to chill out."

"You don't have to be so snippy," Eloise retorted.

"I'm not meaning to be snippy, darling. I'm just trying to tell you in no uncertain terms that time will give you the answers you need and those that are not relevant will probably never be found, that's all."

"I know. I know. It's just a lot to take in, I guess," her voice revealing her exhaustion.

"I can only imagine it would be. Just remember, I'm on your side. I love you," he said gently.

"I love you too, honey. Thank you for always being there for me." Eloise smiled to herself. It had been a long time since Edward told her he loved her. The perfect end to an overwhelming day.

Chapter 8

Edward woke the next morning feeling renewed and refreshed. It was the way he felt when winter turned to spring. New. Improved. Different. Reborn. He got ready for work, went to kiss a sleeping Eloise, and was on his way downtown for yet another busy day. Since going to church at The City of Hope, he sometimes saw some of the parishioners hanging around downtown. Some were looking for a day's work, some panhandling, some just enjoying the day. It was an odd thing to be with a workmate and see one of the unhoused people he knew. He would stop, say hi, and he always asked if he could take them to get a sandwich. It was a natural thing to do in the course of the day if he saw someone he knew. His friends, who didn't understand the many plights of the unhoused, didn't really understand his desire to associate with homeless people.

"You're an easy mark, Eddie," they'd say. "They know where your soft spot is," they cajoled.

Although they knew he belonged to their church, they couldn't resist kidding him when they were in a group, but separately, each told him how wonderful they thought it was he cared so much about people less fortunate than he. But, Edward wasn't looking for kudos; he genuinely loved the people who were, for whatever reason, out in the streets.

Edward wasn't a person who liked confrontation of any kind. He was sure to stand up for what he believed and for the unhoused in his congregation, but he was not a domineering man. He was confident and supportive, knowing he was good at his job in sales and could handle his team and underlings at work. He had an even temper, easy to get along with, but matter of fact. He never had any trouble with anyone at his job and had been in sales for over twenty-five years. His mother had told him he could sell buttons to a zipper company. He was an odd, but likable fellow.

Edward and Eloise met in the checkout line at the grocery store. They struck up a conversation in the line and then decided to stop off at the Starbucks inside the store and have a coffee. Now, here they were, all these years later, still together and while no longer ecstatic as young love generally is, they were happy and content.

Eloise slept until ten o'clock, when the telephone woke her.

"Hullo," she said sleepily.

She heard Gary's smooth-as-butter voice say, "Hey! You still sleeping? It's ten o'clock!"

"Well, I was only sleeping a little bit," she admitted. "Why? What's up?"

"Oh, nothing much. Just wanted to see what you were up to. Anything?"

"No, just sleeping. I've been so exhausted lately and it seems I can't get enough shut eye. But, thanks for waking me up. I needed to get up."

"Sorry," he said sheepishly. "I've kinda been a little nervous about the DNA test and wondered if you were too. I mean, I know basically how it will turn out because I know you are my sister, but I feel very, well, kind of unsettled about it all. Have you had any feelings like that?"

"As a matter of fact, I have. I think that's why I'm so exhausted. I tend to sleep a lot when I'm stressed out or tense. Guess I learned that from Mother. She did it too.

Anyway, I was just talking to Edward about it last night. I was telling him I just have so many questions and no real answers yet."

"What did he suggest?" Gary inquired.

"Well, he didn't really have any suggestions; he just told me that the answers I needed would come in God's timing — not mine. I may not find answers to some things at all. But, that I would have to wait until God was ready to reveal the information. I'd kinda like to help Him along a little bit, though."

"What do you mean, Eloise?"

"Well, when we get the results of the test, I'd like to do some detective work. Find Lulu, find the family Bible, those types of things and see what I can find out. You in?"

"Yep! Sure am. I want to know the answers too and our family is, unfortunately, not the proverbial open book like some are."

"Boy, that's no joke," Eloise laughed. "I used to think our family was pretty straightforward and you know, functional. Now? I'm not quite so sure!" She threw her head back and laughed at her own joke. Gary joined in and they found themselves laughing at the irony of it all.

A few days later, after her walk, Eloise checked her mailbox and found a letter from the DNA lab. She couldn't wait to open it, but she wanted Gary to be with her. She ran in the house and called his number.

"Gary, we got the results! Can I come get you? I don't want to open them without you."

"Sure, Eloise. I can't wait. Come get me and we'll go over to Houndstooth Coffee to read them. What do you think?"

"I can't think of a better idea," Eloise said.

"In fact, I am in great need of a good, stiff cup o' joe. See you in a little bit."

She drove down the highway as fast as she could get away with and of course, with the radio blaring. She was in a good mood and she just knew this was the news she'd been waiting for. The Empire Central exit came up and she took it happily, for once. She soon pulled into the apartment building and as always, Gary was waiting for her. He raised the handle to open the door, but it was locked. Eloise opened the door and he climbed in. She turned the radio down so they could hear each other. They were off to Houndstooth on Henderson Avenue for their coffee and the opening of the envelope. Both were visibly excited and talking a mile a minute.

Eloise was in such a hurry to get into the coffee shop that she tripped and turned her ankle. It hurt, but she was okay. It hadn't turned purple and while swollen, she knew it was just a sprain. She hobbled in, Gary holding her by the arm. She hated being held by the arm, like some little girl who had done something wrong. But, she didn't really have a choice at this point. It hurt to walk and leaning on Gary was comforting and helpful. They ordered their coffee and went to find a seat. Houndstooth was always busy and today was no different. It was a nice day and there were only a couple of people on the patio, so they went outside. When the coffee was ready, Gary went to get them. Since they had been to coffee before, he knew Eloise liked cream and turbinado sugar in her coffee. He fixed it right up for her and added sugar to his coffee too.

They sat across from each other and while Eloise wanted to rip the envelope open as fast as she could, instead, she looked at the man sitting across from her and said, "Here goes nothin'" And with that, she felt the paper in her fingers and opened the letter gingerly. She opened it from the side and blew in to open it wider. It was a trick she learned from her dad. She grabbed the letter, pulled it out slowly, and then opened it to read the results. She skipped down to the bottom where it stated they were twenty-five percent siblings. What did that mean? Eloise looked at Gary, then looked again at the paper, and then she read the results to Gary.

"What does that mean, Gary? 25% siblings?" Gary came around to her side of the table and sat next to her, examining the letter. He looked at Eloise with widened brown eyes and said, "Eloise, this means we are half-siblings! How can that be?"

Eloise was equally horrified, her mouth open and her brown eyes as wide as her half-brother's. "I-I don't know! But, now, I think we have to find Lulu and that family Bible!"

"I think you are right. We need to head to Richardson. That's where Lulu is, but who knows what state of mind she's in." he said.

"Okay," Eloise said. "If the Bible isn't in her room at the Village, where might it be?"

"Gosh, I don't know. I'll have to think about that. She may have some storage facility somewhere. I know she had some friends back in Athens, where we lived, but I don't know if anyone would know where she stored her stuff. I'll have to do some checking around. When do you want to go to Richardson?"

"Well, we need to think this out so that we are not just going willy-nilly, 'round and 'round like a dog chasing his tail. So, let me talk to Edward and kind of make a list of things we need to do first. I'm an expert at list-making," she said proudly.

Eloise took Gary home and then headed toward the house. In the meantime, she called Edward and told him what the letter said. Edward was shocked and said he would have to read the results when he got home from work. She agreed and told him she hoped he could sort it out for her. For now, she would just have to wait.

Eloise made dinner to keep her mind off things. She liked to cook when she was upset or nervous — anything to take her mind off her problem. All the measuring, stirring, and timing the dinner kept her busy and she didn't have time to think about anything else. She thought about calling Danielle, but she wanted to get Edward's take on the results first.

When Edward came in the door, Eloise rushed to him, holding him close. He felt her hot tears on his cheeks and held her tight.

"There, there, honey, it's okay. Tell me what's going on with the results. It's going to be okay. It's all going to be all right."

"I don't understand how we can only be half-siblings. How could that happen?"

"Well, let me look at the results," Edward said as he sat down at the dinner table. He perused the paper and then scoured it for more details. After a few minutes, he raised his eyebrows and set the paper on the table. He breathed in deeply and looked into Eloise's brown eyes.

"Well, honey, it means that you and Gary share 25% of the DNA, which is what makes you half-siblings. The thing is that neither your mom or dad were available to be tested, so there is no evidence of which parent you have in common. One of your parents must have had an affair."

"What?" Eloise shrieked. "Oh my gosh! That's the worst news in the world! Well, sort of. How will I know who it was? Oh boy. This is just too weird... to think one of my parents was unfaithful and after all the lectures they gave me about marriage and fidelity. Wow."

She got up from the table, walked around the kitchen, and sat down again. "I wonder which one it was? I wonder how I find out," she said to no one in particular.

Eloise looked at Edward and inquired, "How do I find out who it was?"

He looked at her quizzically and asked, "Does it matter?"

"Well, of course it matters," she exclaimed. "Of course it matters," she repeated.

While Eloise was happy to have Gary as even a half-brother, she found herself appalled to find out one of her parents must have had an affair. How disappointed, embarrassed, and ashamed she felt of them both. For Eloise, unfaithfulness was against all her beliefs; it was a sin and it was frowned upon everywhere. Secrets. She hated them. *Secrets spelled trouble and hurt every single time. To think anything other than that was just plain stupid.*

Eloise knew that in this day and age people had affairs all the time. But "other people's" affairs did not affect her and her family. She remembered kids who were from families whose parents were divorced and how people would talk to them as if they were pitiful, saying, "I didn't know you were from a broken home."

But, my home wasn't broken.

Edward could see the wheels turning in her brain, knowing her mind was filled with thoughts and beliefs, and that she was brokenhearted. But, he couldn't understand why she was making such a fuss over this. Although, she had loosened up since going to The City of Hope, she still had parts of her that were as staid as the day he met her.

She'll get used to the idea.

After finishing dinner, Eloise decided to do the dishes and watch a movie with Edward. She wanted to wait to tell Danielle what she had found out until tomorrow and of course, fill Gary in on Edward's suspicions.

Chapter 9

Even though Eloise prayed before she went to bed, her night was still long and devoid of sleep for the most part. Thankfully, she fell asleep about three o'clock. Knowing she hadn't slept well, Edward left her sleeping when he got up for work. He usually did, but he wanted to make sure not to wake her, especially today. He hoped while he was spending the day at work, her day would be peaceful and she would be anxious for nothing. He prayed on his way to work for just that. Edward thought about their daughters, Manda and Tessa. They were teenagers, a tough time for girls in some ways and fun in others. With Manda being sixteen now and Tessa, fourteen, he wondered what they would think about all the drama going on with their mother. He felt sorry for them having to deal with more drama than they already had. They were good girls and he never really had to worry about them doing the right thing. But, seeing their mother so distraught always had an effect on them. He prayed that God would sort this mess out and they could go back to the way their lives were before Gary came on the scene. Then he wondered if they would ever be able to go back to what was. Well, either way, he knew God would work it out for them, but it was difficult not to want to help God out just a little bit.

His attention turned back to the girls and the proper way to tell them about Gary and their mom being half-siblings. Manda, the oldest, was a petite beauty like her mom, with brown hair and wide green eyes. She was a little bit taller than her mom, but they looked like sisters side by side. Tessa had a look of her own. She was not the beauty her sister was, but her gentle, sweet ways made up for that. Besides, she was just fourteen and had loads of time to grow into herself.

Edward guessed he would let Eloise take the lead on telling the girls. It was really something she needed to do herself. He decided he would talk to her sometime during the day about telling the girls. Maybe they could do so at dinner tonight. There was no way to avoid the surprise it was going to be to them, but he felt they would take it well and probably embrace Gary readily as their uncle.

Meanwhile, back at home, the first thing Eloise did was pour herself some coffee and get her book of lists — things to do. She checked her email as she drank the black coffee and rubbed the sleep from her eyes. She looked at her telephone and decided to call Danielle. A little early for her liking to talk on the phone, but she had much to do today and she wanted to talk to her friend.

"Hello?" Danielle answered.

"Hey stranger," Eloise said in a flat voice. "I'm so sorry it has taken me so long to get back to you. You won't believe it when I tell you what has happened. Do you have some time to chat?"

"Hey!" Danielle exclaimed. "Of course I have time. I always have time for you. What's up?"

"Oh my gosh, Danielle. It's all such a mess and while I am happy on the one hand, I'm brokenhearted on the other."

"Why? What's happened? Did you find out Gary is not your brother?"

Eloise sighed heavily and said, "Oh, we've found out all right. Are you ready for this? Turns out Gary is my half-brother."

"Half-brother?" Danielle questioned. "How can that be?"

"Well, turns out that one of my parents had an affair and Gary is the result. We don't know which parent since they have both been dead and never told a soul that I know of about this. It is a complete surprise to me."

"Oh my gosh!" Danielle uttered. "How weird is that? And you had no idea anything like that was going on?"

"No," Eloise said. "None at all. Just no clue and I'm shocked and feel as though *somebody* could have or should have told me."

Danielle was curious. "So, what is your next move?"

Eloise put her hand over her eyes and shook her head as she spoke to Danielle.

"Well, I'm going to have to find a way to tell the girls, you know."

"Oh, Eloise, I think that won't be a problem. Your girls are so sweet and accepting, and you really don't have to tell them the whole story just yet. Tell them about Gary and just fill in the blanks as they get older and as you find out more. I mean, you can only tell them what you know, right? And they are smart girls. They know what a half-brother means. That way, you can avoid all the unnecessary details for now."

"Do you think so?" Eloise questioned. "I'm just not sure what to say or why I'm making such a big deal out of it. I guess it's not that big of a deal to have a half-brother, but it feels, well, from my point of view, it feels wrong. I mean, I am not naïve enough to know that marriage vows are sometimes not taken seriously, or that marriages break down for one reason or another, but I never really saw that in my parents' marriage."

"Well, no, you wouldn't. More than likely, they hid it from you and just acted as if all was well when you were around. Right? Wouldn't you and Edward do that if it were you?"

"Hmm, I guess you are right, I don't know. It's weird because I'm glad I have a brother, but unhappy that he's only a half."

"But, Eloise, he doesn't have to be just a half-brother. Don't you see you have the ability to make this relationship what you and he want it to be. Half-siblings are sometimes closer than full. You have the choice to make it what you want. Choose to have the best relationship you can have with Gary. You'll be so glad you did."

Eloise knew she was right and had never really thought of it that way. She was more empowered than she had previously realized. That was pretty cool in itself, but a little scary at the same time.

Eloise also wanted to call Father Don and talk to him about the whole situation. But for now, she needed to get off the phone and get with Gary, either by phone or in person, and figure out what their next step would be.

"Well, Danielle, I have to get off this phone and get with Gary to figure out what we'll do next. I think a visit is in order to this "Aunt" Lulu to see what she can tell us, if anything. She has the beginnings of Alzheimer's, so there's no telling if she can remember anything or not. I'm praying she can remember at least bits and pieces. I'll call you later on when I know something new."

"Okay," Danielle happily chirped. "I feel like I'm in a soap opera," she giggled. Eloise feigned laughter, thanked her friend for listening to her story, and hung up.

"Wow, just wow," Danielle said after she got off the phone. "Some people really do have all the drama."

She smiled to herself and went on with her chores, thinking what a dull life she must have compared to others. No matter. She liked it that way.

Chapter 10

Gary was trying to sleep late this morning. He'd not been sleeping well since the DNA results were revealed. It was troubling knowing he was the result of someone's affair. He wasn't sure why it bothered him, but it did. But, of course, the phone rang, waking him from a deep sleep. He missed the call, but looked at his phone and noted it was Eloise. He wanted to talk to her, but he was just too tired. Instead, he rolled over and went back to sleep.

A couple of hours later, he woke up, grabbed some coffee and called Eloise.

"Hey, Eloise. Sorry I missed your call. I've been so tired lately. Just haven't been sleeping well. How are you?"

"Hey, Gary. Funny you should mention it. I haven't been sleeping either. I slept late this morning too. I don't think I fell asleep until around three this morning. Sorry you are not sleeping well. I was calling to see what kind of action we want to take and when we want to get started. What do you think?"

"Well, we could make a date to go to The Village to see Lulu if you want to. Maybe we could find that Bible."

"Do you have any plans for today? I can go today if you want to. For me, the sooner, the better."

"Well, gosh, I don't know. I've really no plans. In fact, I hadn't planned on doing anything today, if you catch my drift."

"Well, don't you think this is something we should get started on? I mean, it isn't like we have unlimited time with Lulu's dementia and all."

"I guess you are right," Gary said slowly.

"Well, if you don't want to do it today, that's fine," Eloise snorted. "Just tell me when you'd like to do it."

Sensing she was unhappy, Gary relented.

"Okay, we can go today. What time do you want to come out?"

"Thank you. How 'bout two. Lunch will be over at the nursing home and so will nap time. So, we should be in the clear."

"Yep, two is fine. I'll be ready."

"Okay. See you then."

Eloise sauntered into the bathroom and turned on the shower faucets. She needed the hottest possible shower. Her shoulders, neck, and head were killing her, and she knew it was tension. Yes, the hotter the shower, the better. Soon, the steam filled the room and she felt herself begin to relax a bit. Between the steamy shower and an anxiety pill, she felt she would be okay. She wondered what the day would hold in the way of answers. She wished it was Sunday so she could go to church. *Church, though, can be wherever you are.*

After getting dressed and taking her medicine, Eloise grabbed her purse, her keys, a bottle of water, locked the door, and headed for the car. Once in the car, she turned on the radio and cranked up her favorite song. *Yes, church can be wherever you are.* She could feel her head clear as she prayed and sang. She could always trust God to take care of her. She turned off the air conditioner, rolled down the window, and let the wind blow through her hair. She loved the way the wind in her hair made her feel — free, easy, and fun-loving.

Well, she stretched it a bit by thinking fun-loving. But, it was something she would love to be. Maybe, just maybe, she would be one day. She smiled to herself. *Well, you just never know!*

She drove up the driveway to the Kookaburra Apartments. She had to smile; the name reminded her of a song she used to sing when she was a little girl.

"Kookaburra sits in the old gum tree,
 Eating all the gumdrops he can see
 Stop Kookaburra, Stop Kookaburra
Leave some there for me."

Those were such happy times for Eloise. Singing songs, playing games. No worries, fears, or cares. *And no brother.* Her smile faded at the thought.

It sure did seem since she and Gary found each other, she felt whole, as if the other half of her soul had returned. It was an odd feeling.

Gary waited for her with a big smile on his face. Eloise smiled back when he hopped in the car and they took off for Richardson.

Eloise turned the radio down.

"Hey! How are you?"

"Hanging in there and you?"

"I'm doing just about that — hanging in there and that's all," she answered.

"Hey, Gary," Eloise started," do you happen to have a copy of your birth certificate? It would have your parents' name on it and might come in handy in case Lulu is too far gone in her dementia to be of any assistance."

"I had one once, but I have no idea where it might be now. You know, living on the streets, you are prone to lose such things. Not only that, you just don't really think about them. But, I'm sure I could get a replacement," he said.

"Well, why don't you go ahead and apply for a new one and in the meantime, we can be looking for yours. Who knows, it may be in your backpack and you don't even know it. It's funny how things get lost in places like that. I mean, I can carry the smallest purse and still not be able to find my lipstick," Eloise joked.

Gary looked over at her as if she'd lost her mind. *What does lipstick have to do with the price of eggs?* A wry grin came across his face as he thought about Eloise and her analogy. *Ladies are the strangest creatures on* Earth.

Eloise looked at Gary just in time to see the lopsided smile on his face and giggled.

"What's that look for?" she inquired.

"Oh nothing. Just got a little tickled at your analogy." They both laughed the same laugh at the same time.

It didn't take them long to get to The Village. Richardson was a cute little town, but Gary remembered when it was small and doors never had to be locked. It certainly had outgrown that phase in its development now.

"So, Eloise, I'll introduce you to Aunt Lulu and then just let me lead the way. I'm not sure how she's doing and she doesn't know you."

"Oh sure. No problem," Eloise replied. "I wouldn't even know what to ask."

Gary went inside the nursing home and looked for Room 28. Aunt Lulu had a roommate named Shirley Mae, but Gary didn't know if they were still sharing the room. With a bronze cowbell on the door, and the number 28 underneath it, Gary stopped in his tracks. "Guess this is it."

He took one step inside the room and whispered, "Aunt Lulu?"

"If you are looking for Lulu, she's in the activity room playing bingo," someone said.

"Who's there?" Gary asked, the room shrouded in darkness.

"Shirley Mae, who the heck are you?"

"Oh, hey Shirley Mae, it's Gary, Lulu's nephew."

"Okay. Well, like I said, she's in the activity room playing bingo."

He backed out of the room, looked at Eloise, and they went in search of the activity room. They stopped at the nurse's desk and asked for directions.

"Brusque much?" Eloise laughed.

"Well, you know," Gary smiled, "guess there is no real reason to stand on ceremony at their age."

"Guess not," she answered back as they came to the activity room.

The activity room was quiet except for a lady calling the numbers.

"Bingo!" yelled a heavyset woman, with silver hair. Gary looked in the door in time to see Aunt Lulu win the game. A warm smile came over his face and his eyes lit up like a kid's at Christmas when he saw she won.

"Way to go, Aunt Lulu," he said a little too loudly. She looked up and laughed at Gary's remarks. He'd always rooted for her and she for him, so it was only fitting he should be there for her win.

"May I?" Gary asked the activity director, as he walked in the room to help Aunt Lulu up to visit with him.

"Of course you may," the activity director answered back with a smile on her face. It was good to see someone had come to visit Lulu. She hadn't had many visitors since being here. The director sized Gary up in a single glance and watched as he was gentle and loving towards her. She was happy to see that and knew the old woman was happy to see him.

They went to the common area since Aunt Lulu's roommate was in a rather grumpy mood today and they didn't want her eavesdropping.

Aunt Lulu suggested they sit at the dining room table since they could all see each other easily. Gary and Eloise agreed. Eloise let Gary do the talking as agreed.

"Aunt Lulu, this is my half-sister Eloise. Eloise, this is my Aunt Lulu."

Aunt Lulu looked surprised as she said to Eloise, "Nice to meet you, dear. I wondered if this day would ever come."

"You knew about Eloise?" Gary inquired.

"Well, I knew there was another child, but we'd never met."

"Well, we'll get to that after a while, but first, I want to know if you are well and if they are treating you well here? Do you like it? It's not awful, is it?" Gary asked all at once as he was wont to do.

"Naw, it's not awful here. I have several friends and they keep us busy with activities if we want to participate. The food is good and the aides are all pretty decent," she said, using her hands to help her talk. "In fact," she said with a mischievous smile on her face, "I even have a boyfriend."

Gary faked looking shocked and exclaimed, "Aunt Lulu, say it ain't so!" He repeated one of her favorite phrases. Then, they both giggled as if he were a boy again and she, a youngish woman. They talked and teased each other as if no time had gone by since they saw each other last. It was very sweet and endearing for Eloise to witness.

"You seem to be doing better than I had been told," Gary added, "I thought your memory was, well," he looked for a nice way of putting it, "not all it should be."

Aunt Lulu laughed and said, "Yep, the ol' memory makes mistakes from time to time, but I'm not dead yet and there's no sense in trying to kill me off. I refuse to go before my time." She covered her mouth and giggled impishly. "It's true, it isn't always as it should be. I'm on some new medication that helps sustain my memory longer than it would be on its own. So, it helps." Aunt Lulu nodded her head toward Eloise and asked, "How did you find your half-sister? Tell me the story."

Gary was rather embarrassed to admit to his caregiver he had been homeless for a short time and on drugs and alcoholic. It wasn't something she didn't already know, but to admit it was a different and difficult thing for him. As he relayed his past to her, she put her hand on his, letting him know she was there for him, not to judge him, but to love and listen to him. That one little act made him feel safe and secure, and he was able to easily tell the story with honesty. He told Aunt Lulu about The City of Hope service and that Eloise prepared meatloaf — the very recipe his mother used to make — for the dinner after the service. He stopped to ruminate and then began again.

"I was reaching out to Eloise for my dinner when that photo — you know the one, with me and my sister when we were kids — fell out of my pocket. Eloise noticed, picked up, looked at it, and told me I dropped it, then handed it back to me. Later, while I was eating, she came to me, with something in her hand and introduced herself. She asked me who the little girl in the photo was and I told her it was my sister. She then, told me her name was Eloise. Eloise is my sister's name, I said and then she showed me she had the same photo that I had dropped. We knew we were related somehow, but we thought we were full brother and sister. We didn't know until we had a DNA test done that we were only half brother and sister. So, that's one reason we came to see you." And with that, he took a deep breath and blew the air out quickly. "Whew, that was a mouthful," he smiled.

"Hmm." That was all Aunt Lulu had to say at the moment.

And then, "Who would have thought it would have happened like that? Who would have ever thought it would have happened period?" she mused.

Gary watched her think about the series of events and Eloise watched them both.

It's pretty interesting to be the third party to this little drama. I wonder how it is all going to turn out.

"I guess you came here so I could fill in the blanks about things," Lulu said, pushing her silver hair into place.

A grimace came over her face. "You know, this was the part I have been dreading for years. I wish your mom and dad had done this before they died. Brother."

"Well, Aunt Lulu, I know it's not a pleasant task, but doesn't someone have to let us in on the secret? I mean, how else are we to find out?"

"Okay," she said. "Most of the information is in the old Family Bible I left at the storage unit in South Dallas. Go find that and then look through the Bible. It has most of the information there. If you have any questions, just come on back now, hear?"

"Where in South Dallas?" There were lots of storage areas there.

"It's an old place called Your Uncle's Storage down in The Grove, referring to Pleasant Grove. You remember now, don't you?"

"Yeah, yeah. I do," Gary answered.

"Well, this place upgraded to keyless locks, so let me find the piece of paper with the code on it. We have to go back to the room to find it."

By the time they got there, Shirley Mae was nowhere in sight.

"Where do you think Shirley Mae went, Aunt Lulu?" Gary asked politely.

"Oh, who knows? She likes to roll around in her wheelchair and look at the fish. Darn things are boring to look at, I think."

Gary looked at Eloise and both couldn't contain their giggles at Aunt Lulu's comment.

Once Lulu found the code, she gave it to Gary and said, "Do not lose this. It's the only copy I have and I sure don't want to pay for another one."

Gary smiled. "No worries, I won't lose it. I promise."

They stayed a while longer just talking about this and that, and then said their goodbyes to Lulu, promising to be back soon to talk and visit. She kissed Gary's cheek. "You

51

look good, Gary. Now, get a job and live like everybody else, you hear?"

"Okay, Auntie, okay. I'll work on it," he smiled.

After getting in the car and heading out, Eloise and Gary laughed and laughed at the quirky Lulu. Not in a mean way; they were amused and happy to have talked to her. Now they had to decide when they would go to Your Uncle's Storage and look for the family Bible.

Chapter 11

Since it was late afternoon, they decided to go to the storage unit on Monday. They both wanted to have some time to think through their plan, how and what was to be accomplished. Gary would apply for a new birth certificate while looking for the one he'd had a long time ago.

After Eloise dropped him off at his apartment, he rushed upstairs to his computer and brought up the Texas Bureau of Vital Statistics. He filled out the required items except "father." Suddenly, he felt a bit lost since he didn't know now who is father was. He didn't know if he should put Matthew Remick or not. He called Eloise.

"Hello?"

"Hey. I was filling out the birth certificate thingy and I came to the "father" blank. Do I put Matthew Remick there? I don't know now if he was my dad and I have to say it's a really weird feeling."

"Hmm. Gosh, I don't know. I guess just leave it blank. But then, might there be a chance you could be Dad's and not Mom's? I don't know. I guess just fill it out and leave the dad's name as Dad's. We'll see how it comes back. Or, you could fill one out with Dad's and one without Dad's name in the blank and see what happens." And so it was. Gary filled out the birth certificate form both ways.

Eloise couldn't wait to go to church on Sunday. With all that had happened since the luncheon, it felt as if she had not been in ages. True, she had missed a Sunday or two, but she felt more secure now and not so shaken with news of a new brother.

She decided to call Fr. Don this afternoon and tell him all that had happened. She hadn't talked to him lately and she missed it. After God, he was the first one she should have gone to. But, the thing was, she didn't have a problem with having a brother. The shock was one thing. It had pretty much worn off now. What hadn't worn off was the sense of betrayal by their parents, her parents, whatever. She didn't even know how to say it anymore. It used to be her parents. Now, at least one of them is both of their parent. But, who? Only time would tell.

The next day, Saturday, Eloise and Edward did chores around the house. Manda and Tessa had some chores to do as well, but they were still asleep and would be for some time. Eloise didn't mind letting them sleep late on Saturdays. They were generally so helpful around the house and their grades were good, so it was kind of a reward for them.

Even though it was a bit overcast, Edward wanted to work in the garden and scalp the lawn before the winter came in full force. He sure did enjoy working outside. Eloise cleaned the kitchen and sat down to enjoy a cup of coffee. After that, her intention was to dust and vacuum. She wasn't sure it would come to fruition, but her intentions were good. Of course, the road to hell is paved with good intentions, too. At least that's what "they" said. Whoever "they" were. Just thinking about that made her smile.

Pretty soon, two sleepy girls came down the stairs, hair askew, rubbing their eyes.

"Morning, girls."

The two girls returned mumbles in response to their mother's greeting.

"Would you like some breakfast?" Eloise asked.

"No," Tessa said. "Just cereal."

"Cereal is breakfast, silly!"

"Okay," Tessa muttered. "Whatever."

Tessa had a love for Lucky Charms cereal. She would eat it dry, wet with milk, or eat just the marshmallow charms. It mattered not a whit. She loved them over all the other cereals on the market.

Manda didn't care for breakfast and just sat down with a cup of coffee. She was the coffee drinker of the two. Eloise had let her have a little coffee with her breakfast when she was a little girl. More milk than coffee, mind you, but enough coffee to make her love it. She drank it every morning. No more than that.

Eloise wondered if this might be the best time to talk to the girls about Gary. It was just she and them, and it might be an opportune time. She decided it was the perfect time. After the girls woke up a bit, she said, "I want to talk to you girls about something that has come up."

"What, Mom? Is everything all right?" they both said at the same time.

"I think so, darlings. Remember when we made the lunch for the people of The City of Hope?"

"Uh-huh," the girls replied.

"Well, as I was serving the lunch, this man was in line and he dropped a photo. I picked it up and it was the same photo as this one," she told them as she held up the photo of her and her brother.

"Wait!" Tessa exclaimed. "How could he have your photo on him and drop it right in front of you?"

"That's so weird."

"Well, I didn't know. To be honest, I kinda freaked out because that was a photo of me and someone I thought was a cousin." Granny never told me who that guy was, so that's what I thought. So, I went to talk to the guy, whose name is Gary. He told me his mom had given him the photo and the little girl was his sister. Then he asked my name and I told him it was Eloise. He looked at me and said, "That's my sister's name." I didn't know what to say and I asked where she was. He didn't know. It was then I realized I must be his sister. It was some kind of miracle or something. I don't know.

"The problem was I didn't remember ever having a brother. So, long story short, we had a DNA test done. Turns out we are half-brother and sister. What happened, I don't know. All I know is that he was sent away by my dad to a lady named Lulu. They called her Aunt Lulu. I never met her before the other day. She said she wondered when he would find me. So, it appears you two have an uncle and I have a half-brother. Really weird, but kind of exciting, don't you think?"

"Kinda weird is right," Manda said with a question mark on her face. "So, what happens now, Mom?"

"Well, Gary and I have some digging to do to find the truth of what happened."

Tessa lit up like a light bulb, "Mom, does that mean your mom had an affair and he's someone else's kid?"

"Uh, well, that is one theory," Eloise said with a certain uneasiness.

"What's the other theory? Manda asked.

"Um, there is not another theory. But, we have to do some searching for proof."

Eloise knew it had to be her mother who was the connection because the DNA results cited the word "half," which usually indicated the siblings were from the same mother. She was anxious to hear what the story really was.

The rest of the day passed without much excitement. Edward finished up working in the garden and the girls had tidied up their rooms and gone to the mall for the day. All in all, a pretty quiet Saturday.

Chapter 12

Everyone slept in Sunday morning. Since church didn't start until one, it was the perfect day to sleep. The day was on the gray side with a chill in the Texas air. Up by ten, for heaven's sake, Eloise rubbed her eyes and scratched her head as if she was trying to clear her head of the cobwebs that gathered as she slept.

Edward heard her stirring. She was never the quiet one and he began to make her breakfast. "Special breakfast" they called it. It was a breakfast they shared when the girls were little. The girls were never allowed to have "special breakfast" because it was rather pricey and they hadn't had much money back then. "Special breakfast" consisted of lox, bagel, cream cheese, tomatoes, red onion, and capers. It was so good it was almost sinful. Once the girls got older and times were better, they had their first taste of their parents' favorite breakfast. It was as they thought it would be. The girls loved it and asked for it from time to time. But, they knew it was their parents' deal and not their own. Still, an occasional lox and bagel was a treat for them.

When Eloise came into the kitchen, Edward had "special breakfast" waiting for her, with her favorite flowers in a vase on the table. She smiled broadly and looked at him. "What's the occasion?"

"Nothing other than I love you," he said, beaming from ear to ear.

"All right, what's up? This is not at all like you, Edward James Dowager," she jested with a questioning smile.

"Oh, I don't know, just felt like spoiling you a little bit. You've had a... difficult time lately and I wanted to just let you sleep late and lounge around. You know, do nice things for you. I never show you enough how much you mean to me."

Eloise raised her eyebrow. *A bit of an oddity.* She wondered what the real deal was. She decided not to think about it, rather to just enjoy the rarity of the occasion.

They sat and ate quietly. Not about the day, not about the kids, and especially not about Gary. *That's it! He's not mentioning Gary.* She wondered why.

She chose, instead, to bring it up. "I wonder if Gary will be at church today?"

"I dunno, Edward said, not looking up from his paper. Eloise Appreciation Hour was over. He wasn't paying attention to her once again. It was okay though. She got "special breakfast" out of the deal.

Pretty soon, she went back into the bedroom, a place that had become her safe haven, somewhere she could do her own thing and just be. She liked that and while no one really understood why she wanted to hang out in her bedroom all the time, it didn't matter to her — she enjoyed it. It was as if she was wrapped in a blanket, all warm and cozy while she was in there. When she came out, it was as if she had to face the whole world. She wasn't depressed, at least she didn't think she was. She just liked being alone sometimes. She sat in her big blue chair and made notes in her notebook about things she wanted to accomplish during the week.

One thing was to meet up with Gary and go to the storage facility to look for that elusive family Bible. She was anxious to see what treasures lie in that Book, aside from God's Word, of course.

Since they were waiting for Gary's birth certificate, there was not much they could do until it came in the mail. *All this waiting is killing me. I just want to know now.*

Another thing she wanted to do was check out those ancestry websites she'd heard so much about. *I bet while we're waiting, we could find something on one of them.* So, she made a note to check it out and try out the ten-day free trial period. After ten days, she would weigh in as to whether to join the site or not. And there were a few ancestry sites. She wondered if they all had the same information or not.

She needed to go to the store and clean the house. There. Her list was complete, for the moment.

Pretty soon, it was time to get ready for church. She had bought one more pair of jeans and this time, she thought she might wear a t-shirt. That was one of the best things about going to City of Hope, one didn't have to dress to the nines. She wondered who was preparing the lunch today. She had a list of parishioners who were bringing lunch, but she'd absentmindedly misplaced it. Oh, and she did so like to see who was preparing the meal. She guessed that unconsciously, she wanted to see if someone would surpass her meal. She knew it was wrong, that it wasn't the spirit in which the meals were given. It was not a competition after all. But she couldn't help herself. It was just a habit, she supposed. She liked being the best at things — the best cook, best mother, best wife, best housekeeper. That's what her mother had always taught her.

"Be the best you can be all the time. You never know who is watching or who you'll meet when you are out and about." It made Eloise roll her eyes as she remembered her mother's words. She had loved her mother dearly, still did, but man, she sure did have to have everything just so and be just right. She was a woman who never had a hair out of place. *Really? She was me. She turned me into herself. No wonder I'm so stuffy.* She snorted a little laugh and went on about her business. In a minute, she stopped short and thought about how stuffy she had been before going to The City of Hope. She was even wearing blue jeans and t-shirts now, for heaven's sake. She smiled. "Now, that, my dear, is the epitome of un-stuffiness," she laughed aloud.

"Eloise, it's time to go," Edward hollered from the kitchen. "Are you ready?"

Just then, Eloise walked into the room. "Yes, Edward, I'm ready. Are the girls ready?"

"Manda! Tessa! Come on, time to go."

The girls bounded out of their rooms, dashed outside, and jumped into the car.

Edward and Eloise looked at each other quizzically.

"Wonder what that was all about?"

All Eloise could do was shake her head.

It wasn't long before they were at the City of Hope and Eloise, for one, was happy to be there. It seemed like ages since they had been to church, even though it was just two weeks prior. So much had happened in her life and it was a nice respite to come to church, see her people, and hear the Word of God. Today, socks were being given away to the parishioners in preparation of the cold weather ahead. It never got too cold in Texas, but the cold was damp due to the humidity, and it was enough to chill one to the bone. The socks were always a hit, she had heard and now she was seeing the blessing for herself.

Eloise loved to come early to speak to the people and find out how everyone was doing. Some of the unhoused would tell her about the highlights and lowlights of their week. She knew they were learning to trust her as she was learning to trust them. It made her feel warm inside. She hoped they felt the same.

Eloise looked up the hill to see Gary walking toward her. She couldn't quite see his face, but she could discern his sandy locks and his gait from any distance. He had a walk like none other she'd seen before, more of a swagger than a steady gait. It made her smile at the uniqueness of her brother. She excused herself from the group she was talking with, walked toward him, and gave him a big hug.

"I wondered if you'd be here and I hadn't had time to call you," she said excitedly.

"Oh yeah, I wouldn't miss it for anything," he answered back.

"You ready to go in search of the Bible tomorrow?"

"Sure am. I'll be there at nine o'clock with bells on, so you better be ready!"

"Oh, I'll be ready, all right. You be ready!" Eloise said, feigning bossiness.

Eloise called the girls together and putting her hand on Gary's shoulder, said, "Girls, this is your Uncle Gary. Gary, this is Manda and Tessa. Manda is the oldest, sixteen. Tessa is fourteen. She's my baby."

With that, Tessa rolled her eyes and Gary smiled at her.

"Nice to meet you, girls. This whole thing is kinda weird, isn't it? All of a sudden you have an uncle you knew nothing about and I have a whole family I knew nothing about. Yep. Kinda bizarre." By now, he was sure he was talking to himself.

The girls looked oddly at him for just a split second. Their faces softened and they both gave him a hug. It warmed Eloise's heart to see her daughters so accepting of a brother no one knew she had. Suddenly, the whole family was together and Eloise felt an overwhelming sense of happiness and pride.

Father Don presented the homily, which was, funnily enough, on the acceptance of others. Being kind, loving, non-judgmental and Christ-like in our dealings with people. Life was short and it was what you made it. Be kind to one and all; a message worth repeating often.

A fitting sermon for today, a time such as this. It was funny how God always fit the sermon to what she was going through at the time. Of course, it wasn't just about her. Others were going through trials in their lives that the sermon fit as well. Eloise was constantly amazed how the sermons pertained to so many at one time.

It could only be a God-thing. While the Lord's prayer was being said, she looked inward. Eloise wondered if she was as accepting and loving as she should be. Was she as patient and caring as she ought to be? She knew she had changed some, but had she changed enough to make it count? Eloise suddenly realized Communion was being served. She came out of her own thoughts and concentrated on the feast the congregation shared.

She felt whole, something she hadn't felt before and she was sure it was due to finding Gary at her favorite place, The City of Hope.

On the way home from The City of Hope, Eloise could hardly contain her excitement about tomorrow's search for the Holy Bible that may contain the family secrets she hoped to uncover. She could not wait to go to bed, so she could start the next day. It was more exciting than Christmas Eve. Well, in a way. Eloise also felt some trepidation about what she may find out. It was scary to know that her family was not what it seemed to be throughout her life. She wondered if Gary thought the same thing.

Chapter 13

The alarm rang early the next morning. Eloise opened her sleepy eyes and hit the snooze button. Just a couple of more minutes of sleep ought to do the trick. She fell back into a deep sleep and suddenly the alarm rang again. How she wished she could throw it across the room and then she remembered that her day would be filled with searching for the secret that spelled out hers and Gary's lives. She quickly threw the covers back and slipped on her blue house shoes with the fur on the inside. These were her favorite accessory. Her feet were always cold and the fake fur kept them snuggly warm.

She went downstairs and poured a cup of coffee while the girls ate breakfast. The coffee smelled as if it had just been harvested and tasted even better. Eloise had long been a fan of coffee, drinking several cups a day. It was only lately she had started watching her coffee consumption. Even though she loved it, she knew she was drinking too much of it. She attributed it to the increase of panic attacks she'd been having.

It sure did seem funny to be thinking about the cup of coffee you were drinking while you're drinking it.

"Mom, why have you got that goofy grin on your face?" Tessa asked.

"Just thinking about something funny, honey," Eloise laughed at her joke and Tessa rolled her eyes.

"Brother, Mom. You're so weird."

"I know," Eloise laughed, "I like it that way."

Eloise flipped her daughter's hair and walked out of the kitchen. Ready for her shower, her day began just the way she liked it — full of fun.

Soon, she arrived at the Kookaburra Apartments and Gary jumped in the car.

"Hi, Gary. Okay, I've googled Your Uncle's Storage and found the map, so we're off."

"Hey, Eloise! Gosh, you are so efficient!" he laughed. "What else have you been up to already this morning?"

"Well, you know, thinking about coffee and flicking my daughter's hair."

"What?"

"Oh, never mind, just a little joke. Guess you had to be there," she laughed.

"Anyone ever tell you how weird you are?" he laughed.

She laughed with him. Hadn't her daughter just told her this?

As they drove along, they chatted about this and that and didn't delve into anything too serious. The music on the radio soothed Eloise and relaxed her. Eloise's GPS interrupted not only her train of thought, but the song on the radio as well.

"Exit in four hundred feet." And so she did.

It was a beautiful day, a bit chilly, but the sun was out and the sky was the most beautiful shade of blue. Could it be a sign they would find what they were looking for?

After exiting, Eloise turned right and then left into the driveway of the storage facility. It was an old building, with graffiti on some of the units. They drove slowly through the facility looking for 1258. Finally, Eloise and Gary arrived at 1258. Each of them stretching as they got out of the car, Gary found the piece of paper with the code on it and entered the code into the keyless entry. The door clicked open and when they saw the state of the unit, they looked at each other and breathed heavy sighs simultaneously. There was furniture and junk everywhere. That they would have to look through all the stuff packed in there was a daunting task by anyone's standards.

Eloise and Gary looked at each other and finally Eloise broke the silence by saying, "Phew! Where do we start? Do we need a plan?"

Gary looked back, aghast at the sight.

"I think we do need some kind of plan. Are we going to just take out stuff and put it out here or what?"

"Well, that seems as good a plan as any, I guess," Eloise stated.

Since Lulu hadn't told them exactly where the Bible was located, that was really the only thing they could do. So, curiously, they lifted items out of the unit and onto the driveway. There were old clothes, toys, furniture, boxes, and bags. It seemed this was going to take some time, perhaps several days or weeks. But, the two were ready to find the secret of the relationship.

Eloise bowed her head, saying a quick prayer, *"Father, allow us to find all the information pertinent to our parentage and our family quickly so as not to waste time. Lead me to the place where the Bible is located. Amen."*

She was now confident they would find what they needed in its entirety as soon as possible.

An antique roll-top desk leaned against the wall. Gary lifted one end and Eloise, the other. They took it out in the driveway and the top was rolled down. Papers lay on the top of the desk, but no Bible yet. Looking at the papers, it was revealed to be just old mail and nothing pertaining to their little mystery. At the same time, Gary and Eloise were led to a dresser, green with cedar drawers. They pulled out the drawers and a large, beat-up box was in the bottom drawer. Eloise thought this must be the Bible, but when she opened the top, it was just photographs. She took the box of photographs and put them in her car for them to look

65

through later. After showing Gary, neither were sure they would know who any of the people in the photographs were, but they were hopeful that Aunt Lulu would.

Next to the old green dresser was a rich, oak armoire. It was big and beautiful, the grain of the wood smooth and lacquered. Gary saw Eloise running her hand over the top of the armoire and he told Eloise the story of the furniture.

"Our church was having a garage sale and Aunt Lulu saw this armoire. It was painted a putrid green color and the drawers were painted red. Spiders and their eggs took over the closet side of the armoire and it took ages to get all the spiders and their eggs out — or at least it seemed. We decided to buy it and refinish it and upon removing the paint, we found the most beautiful oak finish. Why anyone would cover up that beauty with the horrible green paint. Then, when we stripped the drawers, they turned out to be solid cedar. The smell was heavenly and the color, rich and gorgeous. I was so glad we decided to buy it and refinish it. Whenever I find my own place, I plan to use it. I've always loved it."

"Oh, you should, Gary. It's just beautiful. What did you put on the oak? It's still shiny and lush."

"Aunt Lulu had a thing about tung oil. She loved to use it on the furniture because it gave it a sheen like no other lacquer could. Well, let's look through it."

As they opened and closed drawers, nothing was there to add to their growing pile of stuff to look through. And then, they opened the closet part of the armoire and there it was! A big white and black box marked "Holy Bible." They froze and looked at each other as if they couldn't believe their eyes. The Bible they'd been looking for.

They brushed the dust from the top of the box and lifted the lid. The large family-size Bible was black with gold lettering. Tattered and torn in some places, it told of many nights of being read. This Bible wasn't only on display in their home, Aunt Lulu actually used this Bible often.

Eloise swallowed hard, looked at Gary, and put her hand on his.

"Why don't you come home with me, spend the night, and we'll go through this Bible tonight, tomorrow, and however long it takes to go through it. This is so exciting and I don't think we should keep it in suspense, do you?"

Knowing this was a big move for Eloise, that she would not willy-nilly ask someone to stay at her house unless she knew them well and trusted them completely, he was touched.

"Really, Ellie?" He'd called her that when she was a little girl, but had forgotten until just this moment. She looked at him questioningly, but smiled upon hearing the nickname. Although she didn't really remember him calling her that, it felt and sounded familiar.

She smiled warmly at him and said, "Yeah, really. I'm so excited we found it and sooner than we thought we would, considering this mess." As she said that, her hand circled the air in the unit's direction. It was a mess and they had discussed coming and cleaning it up once they solved their mystery.

As she put the Bible in the car, she hollered, "Let's get this cleaned up and go home. If there's anything else we need, we can look another day."

"Okay, that's a deal!" he yelled back. "I'm beat."

They were there a couple of more hours as they put things back into the unit. They couldn't help but look through things as they did so. Had they not been so curious, they may have gotten out of there earlier. As it was, they couldn't help their curiosity.

Driving home, Eloise looked at Gary and said, "You know, Gary, when you talked about the armoire that you and Aunt Lulu found at the church garage sale, it got me to thinking. The way you stripped away the old putrid paint from that piece is kind of what God is doing to you and me. We've thought our lives were one way our whole lives, or at least my whole life. Finding you has stripped a layer off myself and exposed a vulnerable part of me. Finding out that one of our parents must have had an affair and you were the result is another layer stripped. I think God is planning to strip us down to the bare soul, the bare wood, expose the secrets of our lives and put us back together in a way that is going to be better than what we were in the first place."

Gary looked out the window for a few minutes and then looked at his sister.

"I think you're right. I have to say, I haven't been close to God and I don't pretend to know what's going on here, but you sure have a point. Things are coming to light that I never would or could have imagined. I'm not sure what His plan is, but I definitely think there is a plan in the works."

He smiled at his sister and squeezed the hand that was on the seat by her lap. Never had they been closer than in this very moment.

"I don't know if you feel this way, Gary, but I feel oddly whole. As if a big part of me has finally come together with myself. Does that make any sense at all?"

"Yeah, it does. It's really been that way with me, for sure. It's kind of like they say twins are — whole together and when they are apart, missing a vital part of themselves. It's especially odd for me because I've always felt as if I didn't need anyone for any reason. But, since we found each other, I don't feel like that. In fact, I wonder how I ever managed without you." He paused, shrugging his shoulders, "Well, I guess I didn't manage all that well without you, did I?"

"Well, you did the best you could with what you had. I mean, you had a hard life in many ways. I don't know if I could adjust to being sent off to another person's house and never seeing the people I thought were my parents. That has to be so traumatic." She looked at him with sympathetic eyes. "I can't imagine how that felt and I'm so sorry you had to go through it. But, here we are, trying to catch up and feeling like we are, truly, brother and sister — not half, but whole."

Gary felt hot tears in his eyes. It had been so long since he cried. The last time he cried was because he was so sad. This time, the tears were those of happiness and his soul filled with love and respect for his sister. He never could have believed someone would love him just because he was their brother. Not even a full brother, but half. Yet here they were, whole. The tears were a welcome relief from his past. They cleaned him, heart and soul, and if he didn't know it now, he would soon realize it in full.

Chapter 14

As much as Eloise and Gary wanted to begin searching through the photos and the Bible they found, they were so tired, they decided they would just eat dinner, have a relaxing night, and start fresh in the morning. The day took an emotional toll as well as a physical one. The anticipation of searching for the Bible and the actual searching and discovering it brought a certain fatigue and exhaustion to them both. Edward could see the toll the day took in both their eyes and in their faces. Even though they were elated to have found the photos and the Bible, they were eager for showers and bedtime.

While Eloise took her shower, Edward and Gary took that time to get to know each other.

"Thanks for your hospitality, Edward. I know it was unexpected and Eloise didn't notify you in advance or anything."

"No worries, Gary. I've learned to expect the unexpected with her lately. She used to be so stuck in her ways and, as you know, since we've been going to The City of Hope, everything about her changed. It has been nothing short of a miracle. But, what about you? How are you really feeling about this whole thing?"

"Well, to be honest, it's just weird. I thought I had no one and now I have family who, even though never remembered I existed, now accept me and love me as their own. It's going to take some getting used to, but I have to say, that won't take long, I don't think." And with that, Gary's rich laughter emerged.

Edward laughed with him and said, "I imagine it won't take long at all!" He saw the sparkle in Gary's eyes as he laughed at his own joke and he wondered if he had laughed as easily before. He almost wished he'd known him previously so that he could compare the before and after. He silently bet himself there was a vast difference. Edward really couldn't imagine feeling unwanted and unloved except by an old lady who was no relation whatsoever.

If it were me, I would be devastated. But then, maybe that's all he knew.

Edward was startled out of his own thoughts by the emergence of Eloise, just out of the shower, hair newly dried and coiffed and dressed in her robe.

"Your turn, Gary, if you want to take a shower. Or you can take it later if you want. We never can have two people taking showers at the same time. The water heater just can't handle it! Pretty soon, we're going to have to do something about that, get a tank-less water heater or something. But, for now, it's just one at a time."

She had already shown him his room and he knew he was free to do as he wished while he was here. They decided to watch some mindless sitcom on television so their minds could take a much needed rest. After the news, they all went to bed, worn out.

Morning came in record time and everyone overslept, even Edward. He had to be out and about to get to work on time, but he called in late, opting to take the morning off and go in at noon. He had enough comp time to accomplish this trade out. He wanted to be with Eloise a while this morning, knowing she would be looking through the paperwork and photographs. Edward knew it would be an emotional day for both her and Gary.

"Eloise, why don't we go out to dinner tonight with the girls and Gary? That way you won't have to worry about cooking for all of us after your day of searching for the truth."

"Thanks, darling. I appreciate the thought. That sounds fine and I know it will be a welcome relief later on." She kissed his cheek and whispered, "I don't know what I'd do without you. Thank you."

After a light breakfast, Gary and Eloise retrieved the boxes and looked first at the photographs. There were some of Gary and Eloise when they were kids, but not too many. Two or three of the photos were of their parents, Matthew and Karen Remick and the rest of the photographs were of people they didn't know. They would look to Lulu for answers to these photos.

They opened the Bible and found Gary's birth certificate in a white, legal size envelope. It was yellowed with age and torn in the corner. They carefully took it out of the envelope. The certificate itself was intact, although with some yellowing spots. Mother's name, Karen Remick. Well, that checked out. In the space for the father's name, a name neither Gary or Eloise had ever heard of — Jim Avery was typed in. They looked at each other without a word. The question marks in their eyes was enough and said all that was needed to be said. They set the certificate aside in a pile labeled "Second looks." They would take a closer look at it later, along with some baby pictures of Gary and some other items. The hospital bill for the birth was inevitably left in the Bible's huge, worn pages. As soon as they saw the whopping $86.33 bill for Gary's birth, both their mouths fell open and they laughed wholeheartedly. They could not believe the bill was under a hundred dollars. The bill was subsequently put in a pile labeled "To keep."

They turned the pages slowly so as not to tear the Bible any more than it already was. It was hard not to hurry because of their excitement. It wasn't until late afternoon that they found it, the letter from Karen Remick, their mother. They looked at each other with a mixture of dread and anticipation. Both were nervous at what might be in that letter. The letter was addressed only to Gary. Eloise looked sympathetic and asked him if he would like to read it alone.

"No. No, you are a part of this and I want you to know the minute I do what it says."

"Okay, if you are sure," she answered.

"Yes, I am sure," he said, nervously.

Gary fingered the envelope and finally opened the end of it, just as Eloise had done so many times before. Just like their dad. He blew the envelope open with his breath and gingerly pulled the letter out. He didn't want to tear the paper. He took a deep breath and said, "Here goes nothing!"

Dear Gary,

By the time you read this I'll have probably been long gone for some time. You may not care at this late date why I did some of the things I did, but I'd like to tell you anyway. I hope your life was good and that Aunt Lulu took good care of you. I am sure you'd like to know the story of your life and so here it is. I want you to know the decisions I made on your behalf were because I loved you beyond your imagination. It was my doing you went to live with Aunt Lulu and you'll know why when I am finished with my story.

Before I met Matthew Remick, I had been going steady with a boy named Jim Avery. Jim and I had known each other since we were in elementary school. We had always been friends and in our teenage years, we were very close. He was a tall, sandy-haired man with a smile that could really dazzle. He was a lovely man and I loved him very much. We were young – eighteen and nineteen respectively. I thought we would be together forever when I made the mistake of sleeping with him. After a couple of months, I realized I was pregnant – with you. I thought Jim would be happy, but he got cold feet and he backed off little by little until I didn't see him anymore. I tried to call him, to explain it wasn't just my fault, that it takes two to tango. He was afraid of what people would say, what his parents would say, and I want to reiterate we were very young.

I finally told my parents about the pregnancy and they decided, bravely, I might add, to stand by me. They were so kind and loving, and told me that not one of us had not sinned, and the forgiveness is what the Bible calls for, what Jesus calls for. So, for five years after you were born, we lived with Mother and Daddy and I worked and went to school. School was a rarity for a girl with a child and it wouldn't have been possible without your grandparents. I owe them so much.

Finally, I met Matthew Remick when he came to my workplace to apply for a job himself. We flirted, dated, and fell madly in love. He was everything I'd wanted in a man. He was kind, caring. He loved you and me, and eventually he asked me to marry him. He thought, he said, that he could love you like his own and do right by both of us. And he did. He was a good father to you in the early years. He didn't really know how to be a father, but he did the best he could, you see. Sometimes, he felt like we ganged up on him. If he disciplined you, I would rush to your side and get angry with him without even knowing the full circumstances. You soon learned to play us one against the other and he began to drink, thinking he must be too hard on you and he became more lenient. I don't mean to imply he began drinking because of you. No. He had been a drinker all along, but I didn't know he was actually a true alcoholic until later. He was a confused man, not knowing until Eloise was born what the true ramifications of fatherhood were. He realized how much he missed by not being there from the beginning with you, but of course, that was hardly his fault.

Once you started drinking and using drugs, Matthew thought we'd lost you for good. It wasn't that we didn't want you or didn't forgive you. We did both. But, we had Eloise to think of as well and your bad behavior could not be visited upon her. We needed for you to be a force she could look up to, not a bad influence on her. But, you were not in a place where you could be that for her. That is why I made the decision to send you to Aunt

Lulu's. Lulu was the best friend I ever had and I knew she would take good care of you. She loved you as if you were her own, always had. I owe her a great debt for taking you in when I felt you needed more than I could give. I take all the blame for sending you away. Matthew didn't want me to do it, because he thought I would forever be mad at him and hold it over his head. But, I really couldn't do that, could I? It wasn't anyone's fault. It just was what it was. Both of us loved you so much and were proud of all your accomplishments. You see, we kept tabs on you through Lulu, even though we never saw you after you went to live with her. And I suppose, in many ways, that was not the right thing to do. Looking back, it wasn't the right thing to do at all. I never wanted you to think you weren't wanted, but how could you keep from it, really?

I hope you have found your sister. Jim Avery was living in Mesquite, last I heard, but that was a while ago. In case you want to try to find him, his name is James Paul Avery. I wish you all the blessings in the world and hope you follow your heart. Lastly, I love you with all mine.

All my love,
Mother

By the time they finished the letter from Mother, both Eloise and Gary's faces were drenched in tears. Gary wept for the things he'd never known and Eloise wept out of sympathy for Gary. It must have been, well, it was hard to hear how their mother gave him to Aunt Lulu to finish raising because he might have been a bad influence on Eloise. Eloise felt a load of guilt covering her soul. Because of her, Gary was sent away from his family. Never to see their parents again because they didn't want him to be a bad influence on her. How would she ever live with her guilt over this? Suddenly, she did the only thing she knew to do — bow her head and pray.

"Father," she whispered silently," *give me the strength to bear this burden for my brother. Let him know he was ousted*

75

from our family because of misguided advice from others rather than because of the lack of love for him. I know this couldn't possibly be the fault of the two-year-old child I was, but the lack of knowledge of what to do with an out of control teenager with a drug and drinking problem. Comfort Gary during this time of new awareness and bless his heart during this process. I ask this in Jesus' name. Amen.

As afternoon turned to evening, they agreed to put the Bible up until they had time to absorb the information they had received. Gary's face was fallen and he was deep in thought. After cleaning up the piles of papers and photos, he excused himself to his room. He wanted time to think about this and perhaps to read the letter from his mother again.

He lay on his bed thinking about the time when it was just him and his mom. How they would go to the playground and have a picnic lunch, how he had swung while she pushed him on the swings. He remembered his deep love for her and hers for him. He remembered how happy they were when "they" married Matthew Remick. Gary remembered the times he and "Dad," as he called him, played ball, rode the bike trail together, went to baseball games and football games together. He smiled sadly at his memories.

What he couldn't remember was just why it was he had chosen to partake in drugs and drinking as he did. He couldn't remember what he had thought was so bad about his life that he had to indulge in such behavior. He tried to remember the kids he hung around with, but he couldn't. Those years had been erased by the swirling in and out of consciousness. As he conjured up as many memories as he could, he felt his eyelids become heavy and he fell into a deep, dreamless sleep.

When dinner was ready, Eloise went to Gary's room to find him sleeping. She was unsure whether to wake him or let him sleep. Because she coped with things by sleeping, she knew that was what he was doing too. She tried to reason with herself that he needed the sleep, but he didn't need to sleep too much. She walked closer to the queen-size bed and looked at his face, much more peaceful now than after he read the letter. She opted to let him sleep, rationalizing they could talk in the morning about the shocking revelations of today.

"Is Gary coming to dinner, Eloise?" Edward asked.

"Well, he's sleeping and I know when I get overwhelmed, I like to sleep. It's kind of how I process things and I think he does the same. So, I'm going to just let him sleep until he awakens. I think that may be best for him." And with that, she served dinner to the rest of the family.

After dinner, Manda and Tessa cleaned up the kitchen, then went upstairs to their rooms. It was a quiet night at the Dowager house.

Chapter 15

Dawn broke about five forty-five the next morning and with it, Eloise was already up and about. Odd for her, since she was commonly a late sleeper. She hadn't slept well the night before, worrying about her brother. Normally, Eloise was not a worrier. Not anymore. But, the letter they read from their mother was just so much information all at once. It was absolutely overwhelming to both Gary and Eloise.

She went to Gary's room to check on him, but he was nowhere to be found. She went downstairs to see if he might be in the living room or kitchen, but he wasn't. She ran upstairs and into the bathroom where Edward was shaving his five o'clock shadow and breathlessly announced she could not find Gary anywhere. She was beginning to panic and her first thought was that he'd gone drinking somewhere. She needn't have worried. By the time Edward finished shaving and went downstairs, he spied Gary sitting on the porch swing in the backyard. Edward called to Eloise and pointed Gary out to her. She was relieved, but voiced her fear to Edward about Gary going back to drinking.

"After all," she said, "the letter was quite a shock and it kind of sounded like they no longer wanted to deal with him because of me. I feel so bad about that and you know, I don't know much about alcoholism, but I do know that alcoholics are prone to drink when problems come along and there are feelings brought up that the alcoholic doesn't know how to deal with. You don't think that will happen to him, do you?"

"Eloise, I don't know, honey. We've not known Gary that long, so, we'll just have to wait and see how he handles it all. He may come through with flying colors for all we know."

"I guess you could be right," she said reluctantly, "I don't know either."

Eloise stuck her head out of the sliding glass door and said, "Morning, Gary. You hungry?"

"I could eat, I guess," he replied. "I don't think I had any dinner last night, did I? I think I slept straight through the night, didn't I?"

"Yes, I couldn't bring myself to wake you up. You were so peaceful and there was so much information. I knew you needed to sleep.

It was hard to know whether she should bring it up or not, but she decided to just come out and ask Gary, "Hey, Gary," she began slowly, "I was just wondering if you think you might want to go to an AA meeting sometime today?"

Gary's eyes blazed at her suggestion. "Why do you think I need an AA meeting? I'm not drinking or anything."

"Well, I was just thinking, this is kind of a huge deal and it would be easy to want to drink just at this point. I didn't mean to imply…"

"Imply what? That I'm a drunk, an alcoholic?"

"Well, you are an alcoholic and it can sometimes be difficult to quell the urge."

With that, he stormed off to his room.

Eloise didn't think he would be too happy with her suggestion, but she really didn't think he would get that mad. He was aware he was an alcoholic and so, the thought of an AA meeting shouldn't have upset him that much. But, maybe she tipped the apple cart a little too much. Still, it needed to be suggested.

Eloise went about her daily chores and waited for him to calm down. While she was cleaning her kitchen, it dawned on her she hadn't talked to Danielle in such a long time. A couple of weeks at least. She decided to sit down, give her a call, and catch her up with the latest events. She dialed her number and after three rings, Danielle answered.

"Hello?"

Eloise smiled at the sound of her friend's voice. "Hi! Long time no talk," Eloise laughed.

"Eloise! Hi! How are you? What's new on the Gary front? What have you been up to? I've missed you so much and it's only been a couple of weeks since we talked last."

"I know! It feels like forever since we talked and so much has happened."

"What? Tell me!" Danielle, so happy to hear from her friend, couldn't wait to hear what had been happening.

"Well, Monday, we went to the storage facility where we found pictures, letters, the old Bible..."

"You found it? What all was in the Bible? Tell me everything!"

"Well, after looking most of the day, we found the Bible. It was so late by the time we found it, that we decided to put all the stuff back into the storage thingy and go home to begin to look through the stuff. By the time we got home, we were so tired, we decided to eat, watch some TV, and go to bed. We decided to start first thing in the morning and it was like being a kid at Christmas time, wondering what was hidden in that old Bible. I mean, I could barely sleep. We got up rather early the next morning, as you might imagine, and then began searching for clues. You won't believe what we found out!"

"Was it what you thought? That your mother had an affair? If it weren't for the infidelity, it would almost be romantic."

"No," Eloise said flatly. "It wasn't like that at all. See, Mother had been dating a guy whom she was sure she was going to marry and so she slept with him. It was her first time and she got pregnant with Gary. The guy, scared about the baby and I guess just a kind of jerk, just backed out and they didn't see each other again. Mother was left to her own devices so she told my grandparents. Oh, to be a fly on the wall during that conversation. Anyway, my grandparents were of course, disappointed in her, but were willing to help her out by letting her live with them, putting her through school, and helping her with Gary. Then, she met Daddy. They had a true love story, falling madly in love and marrying. Anyway, it's a whole long story, suffice it to say that Daddy was a good father to Gary, but by the time I was born, Gary was into drugs and drinking and had wild friends. They didn't want me to grow up in that atmosphere. It wasn't Daddy who sent Gary away like we all thought. It was Mother!"

"Your mother sent her own son away? Wow. That had to be hard on her. Was it your dad's idea?" questioned Danielle.

"No! It was my mother's idea. I can't imagine how hard that had to be. She sacrificed her own son so that I wouldn't be subjected to his bad behavior and drug and alcohol use. Turns out Aunt Lulu was her best friend and she loved Gary as if he were her own. She offered to let Gary stay with her and Mother knew he would be well taken care of. She felt Lulu would give Gary whatever it was she was lacking or unable to give him. Daddy had never had his own kid and so it was different when they had me. I have to admit, I've been feeling a bit guilty that just because I came along, Gary had to go live with Aunt Lulu."

Danielle thought carefully about what she was about to say, "Well, the thing is that it isn't your fault. Gary made the choices he made and you were only a baby. It had nothing really to do with you. It had everything to do with what your mother would let influence you and what she

81

wanted you to be around. And she didn't want you to be around that kind of behavior. She really did sacrifice for you and you should really be grateful for that."

"Well, I can see that now, since you put it that way. I wonder, though, if Gary will see it that way."

Danielle spoke swiftly, "But, see, the thing is it doesn't matter if he sees it now. I can just about bet you he will... eventually. As a kind of outsider to this saga, I can see that she sacrificed her own son for a second chance with her family. What I mean is, that not only did she have a chance to raise you in the manner she saw fit, without the drinking and drug abuse, but she gave Gary a second chance at his life with Aunt Lulu. Essentially, she took him away from the people he was hanging out with and put him in an environment with different people and hopefully new friends who did not use and abuse drugs and alcohol. What he chose to do with his life from there was his choice, even at fifteen. He knew he was being sent away for his choices or the lack of good choices and that a baby couldn't be brought up in that atmosphere. I can just about guarantee they explained it to him. Whether he remembers that or not, is a different story. It is okay to feel sorry for him. It would be a hard lesson for anyone, being sent away from the family of origin, but it's not okay to take it on yourself. Do you see what I mean?"

After a long pause, Eloise slid into her words, "Well," she began slowly, thinking about what she was going to say, "I can see what you are saying and I guess you are right. But, can you see how easy it is for me to feel that way?"

"Yeah, I can see how you could feel that way and very easily so. But, it is not healthy for you to take on his transgressions. If you were not related, would you take on his mistakes as easily?"

"No, but..."

"Well, there is no buts, Eloise." Danielle said firmly. "I mean you wouldn't. You wouldn't say, 'Well, it's my fault that so and so did this or that' if you weren't related."

"Okay, smarty pants." Eloise tried to inject some humor, trying to ease her own discomfort. She wondered if Danielle knew just how uncomfortable she had made her friend.

"Well, that is my take on it... as an outsider. As your friend, I absolutely know where you are coming from. I can put myself in your place, but still the fact remains that it is not your fault. It's kind of like, well, let's see how I can put this. You can think of it like this. God sacrificed His Son so that people could have a second chance at life. It's no one's fault God chose to do that; it just is what He chose to do. "

Eloise decided to let that sink in a bit. Even after she and Danielle hung up, she thought about it. She nursed it in her mind and heart and thought about it from many different angles.

Chapter 16

Gary came out of his room, looking for Eloise. He found her in the kitchen with a cup of coffee.

"Is there more coffee, Ellie?"

"Yes, and it's still warm. Want to have a coffee with me?"

"Yeah, but more than that, I wanted to apologize to you for my outburst. I hate that I am an alcoholic and while I hate admitting it, I know I have to. I have to remember the reality of it all. I also want to let you know you are right. I should find a meeting to go to. Do you think you could get on your computer and find an AA meeting somewhere close to here, please?"

"Of course, I can find one for you. No problem. Let's drink our coffee first."

"Ok. I guess there is more to this than I can or, really, should handle by myself. I mean, I have you, of course, but I mean as far as AA goes. I should talk to my sponsor about it. Danny has been my sponsor for a lot of years now and I know he'll be helpful. But, truly, I have no desire to drink... right now.

Eloise looked up at Gary and twirled her hair in nervousness.

"Gary, what do you think our next step should be?"

"Well, I think we should go see Aunt Lulu. She'll be wanting to know what we found out and how I'm doing. That will be the first thing she'll want to know."

"Okay, we can do that. When would you like to go?"

"I don't know, what does your schedule look like?"

"Well, you know me. I'm pretty much open and can go anytime you want to go. Just let me know what you think."

"I think I'll call her and see when she has time to sit down in the family room and talk about all this. I really don't have any questions for her. Our mother pretty much explained everything except why they never wanted to see me again. I would like to know why they didn't."

"Well, I can understand that," Eloise began, "Maybe they didn't want to disrupt the life you had with Aunt Lulu. I feel like they got updates on how you were doing and stuff, don't you?"

"Well, I don't know if they cared to get updates. I feel like they sent me off and forgot about me. I mean, they didn't even tell you about me. So, why would I think they would care how my life was with Aunt Lulu?"

"Well, I can see your point, but I think they must have. Surely, there was no way they could forget you were there."

"I guess not, but doesn't it seem strange to you that we didn't see each other again?"

"It does, but if I know our mother, it had to be really hard on her not knowing. I mean you were her kid. True, she sacrificed for you, but it would seem she would want to know how you were."

"What do you mean she sacrificed for me?" Gary's voice lifted.

"Well, Danielle and I were talking and she suggested Mother sacrificed her relationship with you in order to give you a better life, one without the friends you had been hanging around, one without drugs and alcohol." It had to be painful for her to let you go. I know it was. Just from knowing Mother, I have no doubt she spent nights without sleep worrying about you. She loved you so much that she was able to give you the life you needed in order to kick your habits. With a new baby, she could hardly help you like you needed it. So, she sent you to a place where she knew you would get as much one on one care as you needed. It was all up to you to take advantage of the help she provided through Aunt Lulu. Do you feel you took full advantage of the help she gave you?"

"Well, uh, I don't know," Gary stuttered at his sister's question. "Maybe not. I was only fifteen."

"There ya go. I mean, even though you were fifteen, you knew you were being sent away for a specific reason, right?"

"Maybe. It was such a confusing time and I wasn't sure what was going on. It just felt like I was being sent away from my family for no reason."

"I think teenagers often feel there is no reason for something, but deep down they do know the reasons they are meant to do something, not do something or even go somewhere. Teenagers are often in their own feelings and don't pay attention to what is going on around them. Don't you think?" Eloise stated matter-of-factly. "I mean, look at my own teenagers. They don't necessarily pay attention to things I tell them. They are all about themselves at this age. I could tell them the sky is falling and they would look up and say 'Whatever!' So, see what I mean?"

"I guess you're right, Ellie. I mean, of course I knew the things I did weren't the common things of teenagers — getting drunk and stoned all the time. Sometimes, maybe, but not all the time. I even went to school drunk or high, depending on what I could get."

"So, let's say that you didn't take full advantage of the help Mother gave to you. I wasn't old enough to know what was going on, so you have to be as objective as you can

86

be now that you're all grown up and can look back at it. If Mother had been able to give you all the help you needed with me in the picture, do you think you would have used it to the fullest extent possible?"

"No, probably not," Gary said and continued. "It probably was the best thing for her to send me away. Not only because of you, but because Aunt Lulu did spend one on one time with me and she was wise to my ways. Mother and Dad, not so much. Aunt Lulu kept me busy with extracurricular activities, chores around the house, and other things that had to be done. Of course, it didn't fully stop me from doing the things I had become accustomed to, but it did slow me down."

"Okay, so did you ever pick up the phone and call Mother?" Eloise asked.

"Well, no. I mean, she didn't call me and I guess I never really thought to call her. But, hey! This is not all my fault. You're making this whole deal my fault. "

"Gary, there is no fault finding here. No judgements. We don't really know if Mother called you or not. What if she did and maybe Aunt Lulu didn't think it was such a hot idea for you two to talk to each other. The only way we are really going to find out is to ask Lulu."

"Yep, I guess you are right. But, don't you think it would be weird if Aunt Lulu didn't let me talk to my own mother?"

"Well, maybe, but Mother would have had to sign guardianship over to Lulu so you could get care if you were sick or things like that, so we don't know what kind of plan they had for you. Again, we'll have to ask Lulu. When would you like to go see her again?"

"I think as soon as we can. Turns out, I have some questions that I would like answers to after all. Like, if they had an agreement for me not to talk to Mother, why?"

"Okay, then. Let's go on Monday. That seems to be the day we get quite a bit accomplished, so call Lulu and ask if we can come sometime Monday when she can be alone with us and talk for a while."

"Okay, I'll get right on that," Gary said with enthusiasm.

Soon, Gary was on the phone to Aunt Lulu, setting up a time for their visit.

"I knew this day would come," Aunt Lulu said, "and I thought I'd be ready, but I'm not sure I am."

"No worries, Aunt Lulu," Gary answered, "Nothing will ever change our relationship. I will always love you, no matter what."

"I know, baby. Aw, listen to me calling you 'baby' and you're 63 years old," she mused.

"It's okay. I am still your baby, no matter how old I get," he answered tenderly. He felt she was more his mother than his mother had been even though he and his mom had such a great relationship until he was fifteen. After he hung up, he thought about their relationship. He had known Aunt Lulu all of his life. It was true they had a great chemistry and they truly did love each other. He was proud of her and she was of him, no matter what. He knew he could trust her completely, like no one he'd known before.

Eloise came in the room.

"It's all set," Gary informed her. Aunt Lulu said to be there at twelve thirty. She said she'd skip her nap just for us," and with that, Gary winked at her. She loved seeing the playful side of Gary come out. It was fun discovering all of his moods and his ways.

That night, Eloise decided to talk to Edward about moving Gary to their house. She wanted to be close to him, but she didn't want him to be able to live for nothing. He would have to pay some rent, which meant he would have to get some little job — part time or whatever he wanted to do. Church was tomorrow and she could hardly wait to go. Ever since she had fixed that dinner for the homeless and met Gary and found out he was her brother, she could hardly wait to see what God had in store for her next. It was such a great feeling to love going to church. The sermon was always something timely and she loved how that worked out. It was like Christmas every week for her.

After dinner, Eloise and Edward went up to the sitting room, where they were never disturbed. Eloise knew Edward wanted to read the paper, so she waited to talk to him. She got out her book, *Cemetery Tours*. She had only been reading this book for a little bit, but she was already halfway through it. She felt the genres she loved were a bit of a conundrum when she considered her faith. But, she loved to be entertained and she loved that she could read ghost stories, enjoy them and still believe as she did in her God. She would never let anyone or anything shake her faith or trust in God and Edward knew and loved that about her.

After a while, Eloise broke the silence.

"Edward, how would you feel about offering Gary a room here, in exchange for a small amount of rent? I mean, he's living with some questionable people and he is a recovering alcoholic and addict. He is doing really well while he's here. Do you think that would be okay?"

Edward's eyebrows lifted and his lip curled a bit. He drew a deep breath and exhaled slowly.

"Eloise, really? Do you think that's a good idea?"

"Well, I think it could work short-term, at least while we are working on all this family stuff. I mean, he's paying a small amount of rent on the apartment at Kookaburra while he's staying here. He's been here a couple of weeks now, so..." her voice trailed off.

"I see your point, but are you going to give him a time limit or what are you thinking? I mean, he's a nice guy and I like him and all, but it might get old after a while, don't you think?"

"It might, but I don't think it will. We've only just been reunited and I think it would be okay. We could say it could be a six-month time period or so. That way, we should have all this wrapped up, unless he wants to find his father or something. Then, we'd have to renegotiate." She batted her eyes and added, "Please, honey. It could be fun and he does stay pretty much out of the way and he helps around the house a bit. What do you think? Can I ask him if he'd like to stay?"

"Oh Eloise, when have I ever been able to say no to you?"

She jumped up and down and clapped her hands together. Her eyes danced with excitement and Edward knew he'd done the right thing. Eloise tried to be calm and collected when she ran downstairs yelling, 'Gary!!!'

Gary came toward the stairs, looking at Eloise questioningly. "What is it, Ellie? Are you okay?"

"Oh, yes, everything is fine, but I have something to ask you. Let's go sit down."

"What is it?"

"I was thinking, Gary, what do you think about moving in here for a while, at least while we are working on all this family stuff. I was thinking you could get a little part time job and pay a small amount of rent so you would feel a part of the family. Anyway, you are paying for the Kookaburra apartment and you're not even there. Might as well just stay here. What do you say?"

"Wow, Ellie, that's a pretty big deal. I mean, I know how you are about your privacy and all. Are you sure this is something you want to do? That you want to even consider?"

"Yes, I do. I have and I think it's the perfect solution; we don't know how long this will go on and there is something I've not yet asked you. Do you want, I mean, are you thinking you might want to look for your real dad?"

Gary looked shocked. "I've not even thought that far, Ellie. What would make you think I want to find him though?"

"So you will know who you are, unless you are okay with just knowing about Mother."

"I bet he's not even alive anymore. And if he is and I found him, well, what about it? He probably wouldn't even remember."

"He might not, but you would be there, in the flesh, to remind him. I mean, really, he could have stuck around to get to know you, even if it was just a little. I don't know, maybe that's my deal. Maybe I'm mad because he didn't stick around for you, that he didn't give it a chance. You deserved a chance!" With that, Eloise's face was flushed and her voice went up about a half an octave. This was the first time Gary had really seen her angry. She often had trouble accepting injustice. It just made her angry to hear of any. But, injustice was everywhere. And this was her brother, so it really did hit home with her. She wanted it to hit home with him. It was, after all, his life. She tried to stop her thoughts. His life. It was his life, not hers to make decisions for. After all, he was a big boy and he could make his own decisions.

"I'm sorry, I forget that it's your life and you should be the one to make decisions for yourself. I shouldn't interfere." And then she was quiet.

With that, Gary said, "Why don't we sleep on this? You may change your mind. I would love nothing better than to stay here with you, but I also know how you are about your privacy and your family. They are very dear to you and I don't want to be the reason you feel squeezed out of your own space."

"Okay, but I won't change my mind. We're in this together. By the way, you going to City of Hope tomorrow?"

"Oh, yeah. Absolutely! Wouldn't miss it."

Then they went to their separate rooms.

Chapter 17

The night went faster than usual or at least it felt that way and no one wanted to get up Sunday morning. It was a good thing church didn't start until one in the afternoon, so they were able to sleep. It was unusual that they all came downstairs about the same time that morning. Cereal came out of the pantry, milk out of the refrigerator. The smell of toast cooking in the toaster wafted through the house. The brilliant coffee aroma filled the kitchen with that fresh picked coffee bean smell. Perfect for a lazy Sunday morning.

After breakfast, Eloise turned on the Christian radio station she loved so much to get her heart ready to accept what God had to say to her today. She felt it would be a good message and she knew it would be timely. Eloise closed her eyes, sitting back in the chair, and sang along with the radio at the top of her lungs. Edward loved watching this ritual of hers. She loved listening and singing to the radio, especially just before church. It really prepared her heart for the service.

Once they got to The City of Hope, they saw the old friends, but this week, there were new faces as well. The homeless were not always very talkative the first few weeks they came to City of Hope. Trust didn't come easy and Eloise, along with their friends Danielle and David, greeted those in attendance. This was their favorite thing to do, to connect with those who worshipped there regularly and those who were new. It was a chance to really listen to what they had to say, forge new friendships, and to build the trust that was so needed.

Soon, all were seated and the music began. The liturgy books had been passed out and all followed along.

"God is good all the time!" The congregation responded, "All the time God is good!" It was a rousing way to start the service, to remind each other how good God is, and faithful all the time. Everyone loved to say it as loud as they could, as if announcing it to the world, their world, and their inner selves. Life on the streets is not easy, but this reminded the people they were not alone in their ventures.

The scripture was Matthew 12:48 which read:

"While Jesus was still talking to the crowd, his mother and brothers stood outside, wanting to speak to him. Someone told him, 'Your mother and brothers are standing outside wanting to speak to you.'

He replied to him, "Who is my mother and who are my brothers? Pointing to his disciples, he said, "Here are my mother and my brothers. For whoever does the will of my Father in heaven is my brother and sister and mother."

With that, Eloise looked at Gary and he looked back at her in amazement. Gary's eyes filled with tears with the newfound knowledge that Aunt Lulu *was* his mother since she was doing God's will in helping to raise him when his parents no longer could. God had given him two sets of parents to look after him, teach him about God and the things he needed to know in preparation for life and for finding his sister. They taught him, indirectly, how to deal with the surprises in his life. Although he was a recovering alcoholic and addict, he knew just at this moment that he would have to find his birth father, James Paul Avery. He hoped his dad was still alive so he could find out what kind of man he was. He suddenly was no longer angry with him; he was, instead, curious and had tender thoughts about his birth father. He didn't feel the grinding animosity he had felt when he read the letter from his mother. He broke from his thoughts when the Lord's Prayer was being said. He joined hands with the rest and said it with them. He couldn't explain what he was feeling at that moment, but it was a quiet peace he'd waited for all of his life. He decided he would think about how he was feeling and embrace it with all he had. Communion, today, had taken on a different meaning for him and he couldn't wait to talk to Eloise about it all. He wondered what she was thinking. He looked at her, taking her hand and squeezed it tightly.

After the service, Eloise, Gary, and Edward sat together eating lunch quietly. No words were needed.

When they got back to Poetry, it was four o'clock in the afternoon. They'd spent much of the time talking to parishioners and helping to clean up. They were all physically and emotionally worn out and each one went to their rooms to rest.

The sermon had touched each of their hearts and it amazed them, the timeliness of it all. With Gary just finding out about his dad not being his real dad and Aunt Lulu taking the place of his parents at the tender age of fifteen; it was a lot to take in, to think about. But, the sermon made it clear that Lulu and Gary's stepdad, Matthew Remick, were fulfilling their God-given duties as his parents, whether they knew it or not. He was fortunate in that he had three people who acted as his parents throughout his life and one was still alive. All of them had cared about him and touched his life in their own way. Yes, he was a fortunate man.

Two hours had passed and each of the Dowagers had begun to come out of their rooms, well rested and ready for dinner. They decided to call out for pizza and take it easy the rest of the evening. Tomorrow was the day Eloise and Gary would talk to Aunt Lulu. It was going to be an emotional day, that's for sure.

In the meantime, they sat around the television, eating the piping hot vegetarian pizza, commenting from time to time about how good it was. They watched *Downton Abby* on the public television channel and loved every minute of it. It was their favorite show and this, the last season was the most exciting one yet. Sunday night was traditionally British Comedy night, but the local PBS station had added more detective shows to its lineup than it had comedy. The Dowagers were much chagrined about that, but there was not much they could do about it. Beside *Downton Abby*, they watched one of the detective shows. Otherwise, Sunday night television was a bust.

Chapter 18

When the Dowagers woke up the next morning, it was muggy and hot — perfect conditions for a storm. The sky was dark and the clouds looked angry. Appropriate weather for confronting Aunt Lulu with all of Gary's questions about his past, questions about his life with his parents and with her. Eloise wasn't sure she should really sit in on it all. She thought Aunt Lulu might not talk openly about their mother and Eloise's dad. She didn't want to take anything away from what Aunt Lulu might say if she were absent from the room. But, Gary wanted her to be there. It was almost as if he were afraid of what she might say. He just needed some moral support and Eloise was just the one to give it to him. She had really enjoyed her time with Gary and hoped that he would come stay with them for a while. Even if only a short time. They had both grown used to leaning on the other from time to time, when it counted. After all, they were all of the family of origin they had. Just each other. Sure, Eloise had her family, but that was more like an extension of her and Gary liked that about them.

After Edward left for work and the kids were getting ready for their day, Eloise and Gary were getting ready to go to The Village to see Lulu. The girls were to spend the day cleaning the house. Of course, they grumbled about the chore, but they had both been so busy lately, it would be nice for them to stay home for a change. It was summer, though, and there was always something to do. They could go swimming when they were finished with the house, perhaps.

Gary sauntered into the living room, and saw Eloise grabbing her purse, slinging it over her shoulder.

"Ready to go? I sure hate driving in the rain," she mumbled. She'd had a wreck once during the rain and since then, she'd been afraid to drive in it. But, this was an important errand they were on and she couldn't say she didn't want to drive just because of the rain. Gary didn't have a license currently, so she was the only one who could drive. She took a deep breath in and exhaled very slowly.

You can do this, you can do this. It's only driving. Something you do every day.

She thought about turning the radio on, but she wanted her full concentration to be on the road. This was no time to have an accident.

"Ellie, I'm kinda nervous about talking to Aunt Lulu about all this."

"I know. I'm a little nervous for you, but how bad could it be? I mean, it's information you really need to have. It's about time you knew all the details, you know?"

The rest of the drive was rather silent, only the occasional comment said. Both found themselves in thought wondering what today would bring, what details would be spilled. Soon, they would find out.

About twenty minutes after commencing their journey, they arrived at their destination. The blue banner above the door announced where they were: The Village. The area outside was landscaped beautifully with irises, sunflowers, and varying bushes. Whoever landscaped it sure knew what they were doing. It was beautifully done.

A new fish tank had been installed near the front door. One could see it as soon as the door was opened. A tank full of beautiful neon betas was displayed for all to take in. Eloise always saw fish tanks in the dentist's office and she knew they were there to entice people to relax. Since it was in her dentist's office, it never caused her to relax. Instead, it made her think of all the fillings she'd gotten. She laughed to herself at the memory.

She and Gary sauntered down the hallway to Room 28, where Aunt Lulu would be waiting for them. When they got to her room, she stood up and embraced Gary and held out her hand to squeeze Eloise's hand. She wore a flowery pink house dress and her hair had just been cut and curled. She looked much younger than her years. Secretly, Gary hoped today was among her good days. He needed her memory to be clear. Just today. Please God, let her be clear.

"How are you, honey?" Aunt Lulu inquired.

"Pretty good, Aunt Lulu, and you?" Gary asked.

"Oh baby, you know, life has its ups and downs, especially at my age," she laughed.

"I know you found the Bible and you have some questions. Did you see anyone in the dining room when you passed by?"

"I do," he said, "and no, I didn't see anyone in the family dining room. Shall we go check it out?"

"Sure," Aunt Lulu said with a strong voice.

Gary wondered if she dreaded this question-and-answer session with him.

"Well, honey, I knew this day would come, when you would want to know what had gone on while you were a young 'un," Aunt Lulu told him.

"I wish I'd known there was a day coming. I have to say, I feel a little blindsided by it all. Couldn't you have given me some kind of hint about what was going on?" Gary interjected.

"No, I promised your mother I'd not tell you until you came and asked me. Your mom never wanted you to feel as if no one loved you; there is nothing that was further from the truth."

They walked to the mahogany table and sat down, Gary sitting across from Aunt Lulu so he could see her dark eyes while she told her story and answered his questions. He was always able to tell her true feelings by looking into her eyes.

"Where do you want to start?" Aunt Lulu asked.

"Well, I'd like to start with the fact that James Paul Avery was my real father. Did you know him?"

"Well, yes and no. I was not around him much, but I did meet him. He was a nice enough man, I thought, but then when he found out your mom was pregnant, man, he headed for the hills. It just scared him to death. No one really knew why, though. He was a handsome man, dimples and the same color sandy hair as you. He was tall and lanky, and kind of shy and awkward."

"Do you know if he is still alive, Aunt Lulu?"

"No, can't say as I do," she answered, "Why? Are you looking to try to find him?"

"Aw, I haven't really decided yet, I mean, he never took the time for me, but I still want to know who he is, what he looks like. Does that make sense?"

Aunt Lulu looked slightly worried as she considered the possibility of Gary looking for Jim.

"Well, I suppose there is a certain amount of curiosity surrounding Jim, yes. It makes sense. Still, don't wear your heart on your sleeve. Be aware he may not want to meet you. I can't imagine anyone not wanting to know you, baby, but it could happen," she said.

Gary rubbed his chin. "Yes, I am aware of that, but still, there is something inside of me that wants to find him. And yet, there is part of me that never wants to find him. It is all sort of confusing."

Lulu patted his hand and covered it with her own.

"I know it must be, Gary, and I'm sorry you have to go through this mess. But, we all have our crosses to bear, don't we?"

"I guess," was all he said. He got up from the table and walked around the room. "Aunt Lulu, can you tell me

99

more about when Mother asked you to take care of me? What did she say and why did she never visit? We were so close once upon a time and for her to never see me again, well, I just don't understand why."

"I know you don't. I never really understood it either, but that was the way she wanted it. She called me one day after you had gotten into some kind of trouble. I can't remember what you'd done, but it was fairly serious. Anyway, she called me and told me she had no new ideas about how to handle you. She cried and said she couldn't take the chance you would unduly influence Eloise as she grew up. Had your mother not intervened and brought you here, you'd have been in jail for sure. You had just gotten so out of hand. So, I took you in and it was never a problem. It was my joy as I couldn't have kids of my own. But, we had to get you back under control. Baby, that sometimes takes someone besides your own parents. Your mother was so distressed at having to send you here, she didn't think she could cope with coming to see you, but not being able to take you home. Her heart was just broken. She didn't mean for you to think she didn't want you, but what else were you to think, really?"

As Aunt Lulu took paused to take a breath, Gary said, "I just couldn't get along with them after a while. They were always after me and sometimes, yes, I had done something wrong, but the times I hadn't, they still made out like I was the bad guy. I felt like I just couldn't win, but in some odd way, I don't blame anyone but myself. Still, I have some anger left. So, I'm kind of stuck in the middle."

"I know this must be very confusing for you. I can't tell you what was in your mother's mind other than getting you the help you needed and she knew I could help you. She couldn't bear to see you and have to leave you, even though I would have preferred that to not seeing you at all. She was a flawed, broken woman in many ways. I'm not making excuses for her, but I am trying to help you see her in a way she would want you to. She had flaws. We all do. But we do the best we can with what we have. Do you know what I mean?"

"I-I guess so. But, why didn't you tell me all this stuff before now? Why did I have to find out on my own? It really left me feeling like no one cared, not even you."

"Your mother left me with stipulations that she put down in a legal document. I was not to tell you about any of this unless and until you asked me about it. It was a part of the guardianship stipulations. I had to abide by them and only talk about this when you asked. Had you never asked, I would have been obligated not to tell you. I'm sorry I ever agreed to it. At the time, though, it made sense and I did it for your sake. I hope you can forgive me."

"I understand you did it for me, but it makes me angry that stipulations existed in the first place. I feel like this is all my fault, but it couldn't be, could it? I was just a kid, for heaven's sake."

"No, Gary, there is no direct fault here. The fault was both yours and your mother's. But, there is no sense in talking about whose fault it was or wasn't. It's done and in the past. The best thing for you now is to take your life from this point on and make it the best you can. As John Wesley used to say, 'Do all the good you can for as long as you can.' When you do that, you have made things right for you and everyone who knows and loves you. You see?"

"I do see, Aunt Lulu. I finally see."

Afterwards, Gary was satisfied with Aunt Lulu's answers and had no more questions for the time being. They cut the visit shorter than they had anticipated and bid a fond farewell to the old lady who watched them walk out the door with a smile on her face.

I'm so glad that's over with, at least for now, Aunt Lulu thought as she watched them drive away. She knew he'd be back with more questions.

Chapter 19

Gary had been lucky getting such detailed answers from Aunt Lulu considering she had onset dementia. Things however changed with a phone call at seven the next morning.

"Hello?" Eloise answered sleepily.

"Is Mr. Gary Remick available? This is the Village."

"Oh, yes. Just a moment please."

Eloise plodded down the hall to Gary's room to wake him. He was lying in bed, awake to her surprise.

"Gary, the phone, it's for you. It's The Village."

"Oh no, not this early in the morning," he muttered.

She handed him the cell phone and he quietly said, "This is Gary Remick."

"Uh, Mr. Remick, this is Estelle from The Village. Your Aunt Lulu has had a stroke and has been taken to Holy Mary Hospital. Can you meet the ambulance up there?"

"Of course I can. I'll leave right away. Thank you for calling."

"Eloise! Aunt Lulu has had a stroke and she's at Holy Mary Hospital. Can you take me there right away?"

"Of course, let's get dressed as fast as we can."

And they did. Soon they were off to the hospital which was about fifteen minutes away. By the time they got to the hospital and came through the door, they were told Aunt Lulu had had another stroke and the outlook wasn't good. She was not expected to live. Sadly, Aunt Lulu passed away that afternoon. She lived just long enough to give Gary the answers he so needed to sort out his life.

Gary couldn't believe she had died. His rock throughout life was gone. He was so sad and yet, he couldn't cry. He realized she had been put on this Earth to be his mother according to God's will and she lived just long enough to give him his life back. He couldn't be sad about that, but he was heartbroken he wouldn't see her or talk to her again.

In the meantime, Eloise was so shocked at Aunt Lulu's demise that she shed a few tears. She was so sad for Gary and wondered if there were any other details Aunt Lulu might have been holding on to. Well, there was nothing to be done about it now. There was, however, a funeral to plan and attend. After that, who knew what the next few days might bring. She called Edward and told him of the sad news.

"No way!" Edward exclaimed. "She died? How bizarre is that? Right after giving Gary the answers. Has to be a God thing. Has to." Edward rubbed the back of his neck, shaking his head.

Gary had Aunt Lulu's body sent to Younger & Sons Funeral home. Per her request, she was to be cremated and just a small memorial service was to be held. Gary was to meet with the funeral home at three o'clock to sort out the details and set the service. He asked Eloise to come along because she was so good at covering the small details. He was never any good at that part of things. Besides, his head swirled with her sudden death. He couldn't imagine his life without her. True, he had not always kept in touch, but he knew she was there if he ever needed her. Now, well, now, she wasn't and never would be again. He could hardly bear to think of it.

Two days later, Gary and the Dowager family went to the little memorial service for Aunt Lulu, Gary's second mother. Gary hadn't known when his real mother died and this, to him, was a double death. He mourned both his real mom and his second mother and he was simply overwhelmed. The tears fell freely and unashamedly from his eyes. It was a lovely service and some of her old friends had come, many of whom Gary didn't know. He looked around the room and realized Aunt Lulu had quite a few friends. That warmed his heart.

After a few words were said and *How Great Thou Art* was sung, her minister announced, "There will be a reception, if you care to stay a few minutes, in the Fellowship Hall. When you go out of the chapel, turn right and it will be directly on your left. The church has prepared a luncheon in honor of sweet Ms. Lulu. The family wishes to express their great appreciation for your attendance today. Let's all sing *Amazing Grace* and be dismissed."

After the hymn was sung, people began to leave and Eloise looked at Gary. "Shall I leave you a while?" she asked him.

"Yes, please do. I just want to sit here with her for a few minutes if you don't mind."

"Okay, I'll meet you in the Fellowship Hall."

"Okay," his voice trailed off. He continued to sit in the uncomfortable pew and watched while the people filed out. All but one.

An older man went to the altar, where the coral and cream-colored urn sat. Gary had never seen this guy and wondered who he was. Finally, his curiosity couldn't take much more and he decided to introduce himself.

He walked up the aisle toward the urn in his unique swagger, and said, "Did you know her well?"

The man looked at him intently with steely gray eyes.

"Once upon a time," he said slowly.

Gary thought he must be just a bit older than Aunt Lulu had been. He stretched his hand out.

"Gary Remick"

"Jim Avery."

Acknowledgements

I would like to thank my mentor, Jacqueline E. Smith, for guiding my way through the publishing process and for being such a great friend to me and my family. Thanks to my husband, Stephen for listening to each chapter and adding his input. Many thanks to Sue Soares, my editor, and of course, I couldn't have written this without God's help.

PAULA D. WALKER BAKER was born in Dallas, Texas and raised in the nearby suburb of Richardson. She attended Richardson High School and later, Texas A&M Commerce. Paula has three children and five grandchildren. She currently resides in Royse City, Texas with her husband Stephen and all their animals. Paula is also the author of the JACK LEARNS children's book series.

www.ingramcontent.com/pod-product-compliance
Lightning Source LLC
Chambersburg PA
CBHW021132020426

42331CB00005B/730

*9 7 8 0 6 9 2 7 4 2 2 0 4 *